Author   WARREN

Title   Lester Horton

lester
horton

lester horton

modern dance pioneer

larry warren

marcel dekker inc.   new york and basel

Cover design elements and chapter opening figures are from original sketches by Lester Horton. Alvin Ailey quotation reprinted by permission of *Dance News* (April 1976).

MARCEL DEKKER, INC.
270 Madison Avenue, New York, New York 10016

Library of Congress Catalog Card Number: 76-23364
ISBN: 0-8247-6503-6

Current printing (last digit):
10 9 8 7 6 5 4 3 2 1

Printed in the United States of America

To The Memory of My Brother, Bern

contents

foreword — *John Martin*   vii

preface   ix

acknowledgments   xiii

illustrations   xv

the life and work

a regional theater is born   3

young man goes west   21

salome dances   45

dancers unite!   57

interlude   103

dance theater   115

rebuilding   147

new york   181

notes and sources   193

for the record

horton on dance   201

program notes   215

scenarios   225
talking about horton   231
et cetera   239
chronologies   243

index   257

foreword

That art grows out of the necessities of its environment is incontrovertible, and outside that environment and those necessities it can evoke only objective responses. On this basis, to be sure, our expensive international cultural-exchange programs would seem to be on the wrong track, and perhaps they are; instead of bringing over to us the Bolshoi Ballet, say, it should be sending us, or generous portions of us, to Moscow. Only that way can we grasp the urgent values of art, since the audience for which it has been made constitutes a part of the experience itself. You have only to sit in one such audience to realize how deeply its response is its own.

It is important, then, if we are to have any conception at all at this late date of what Lester Horton's art was like, and how it came to be that way, that we hear it from someone who was part of that audience.

During his lifetime, indeed, Horton's work was virtually unknown east of Pasadena. In the East we were turning cartwheels over Graham and Humphrey and their colleagues, altogether unaware that somebody was breaking similar ground on the West Coast and with comparably revolutionary results.

It may well be that the mountains and the desert, the Great Plains and the badlands make California more remote from New York than the Atlantic makes Europe. When you fly over the ocean, Europe is the next stop, for there is nothing in between but water; when you are flying to California, you are flying over all kinds of geology where all kinds of people are making all kinds of individual cultures. And when you have finally crossed the Great Divide, have found that all the rivers run the other way, that the ocean is with good reason named Pacific, and the year has no seasons, it becomes clear that a guide, an interpreter, who speaks both languages is essential.

Having studied and performed on the West Coast before teaching in the East, Larry Warren comes to us as that bilingual interpreter. Because he knew Horton's work in his most impressionable years, experienced it deeply, and was in a large measure shaped by it, he can give us a first-hand account of it and the people associated with it, a subjective interpretation; because he has lived and worked in the East, he can give us a historical perspective on Horton's work, an objective evaluation.

It was inevitable that Larry Warren should have written about Horton, given "faces," as it were, to the people he has written about, and brought forth this valuable book.

John Martin

preface

It is time to set the record straight — time to look at Lester Horton's achievements and contributions to modern dance, passing over the standard considerations of what *might* have happened had he chosen to work in New York, and setting aside the damnation with faint praise which appears to have become an intrinsic part of the formula for any discussion of Horton's life accomplishment in dance. The title of one such discussion, Clive Barnes' "Genius on Wrong Coast,"* characterizes the attitude of most Eastern critics and therefore helps to explain the need to "salvage" Horton's reputation. That his reputation should need rescuing at all seems inconceivable, since he stands with Martha Graham and Doris Humphrey as one of the three American teachers whose methods have established influential schools and whose choreographies are being revived as modern dance classics.

But Lester Horton had chosen to do his work in Southern California, three thousand miles away from the capital of the modern dance world; and Los Angeles, his home base, was regarded as a bush-league city, notorious for its lack of serious art. It was assumed that nothing original or important could come out of Hollywood and that Horton must, therefore, be attempting to emulate the work of Graham, Humphrey, and

* *Genius on Wrong Coast,* syndicated in *Los Angeles Herald-Examiner,* December 3, 1967.

Wigman, a charge he was plagued with during his entire professional life. Even when they praised him lavishly, Southern California critics, unable to conceive of an original talent in their midst, too often wrote about him as a pretender to Eastern thrones, and writers in the East were happy to accept their colleagues' evaluations, seemingly anxious to preserve their belief that New York had the only dance of any importance in America.

Horton's casual, offhand manner with interviewers no doubt contributed to his neglect by the press during his lifetime. Where other pioneers in modern dance understandably did what they could to enhance their reputations, maintaining a cool aloofness and an atmosphere of exclusiveness around their studios, Horton's almost obsessive democratic spirit would not allow him to set himself apart from the rest of society or to accept any deferential treatment as an artist. Like his contemporary, Charles Weidman, who also came from the American prairie, he often spoke lightly of his own accomplishments to focus greater attention on his dancers and other collaborators. Unfortunately for his reputation, the press took him at his word.

Often, too, the critics who accepted Horton as an original tended to fault his playfulness, not recognizing that the artist's capacity to be fanciful in his work, his excursions into theatricalized ethnic dance, and his delight in form and color were intrinsic to his creative process. Had he worked in New York he would perhaps have been forgiven his occasional excesses for the sake of his inventiveness.

The roster of artists he trained should alone assure his place as a prime contributor to the mainstream of the field. Among those were Bella Lewitzky, whose phenomenal career has spanned forty years of dancing, choreographing, and innovative teaching; Carmen de Lavallade, who has had a distinguished career as a dancer; James Truitte, one of America's outstanding modern dance teachers; Rudi Gernreich, an innovator in the fashion industry; and

Alvin Ailey, who leads one of the world's best-known dance companies. There are, of course, many others, including James Mitchell, Janet Collins, Carl Ratcliff, and Joyce Trisler. Through all of these artists and more the work is still going on. Horton's exuberant, free-flowing training techniques are now being taught in cities throughout the United States, and the full impact of his career is yet to be known.

The very existence of the Dance Theater Horton created and to which he gave his enormous talents during the last five years of his life places him among a rare breed of pioneers in regional theater, and the fact that it was a theater exclusively for modern dance underlines his courage and originality. In those years modern dance was still regarded by many as an esoteric recital form, and few had as yet seen its possibilities as total theater.

7566 Melrose Avenue, Hollywood, California is now the home of a gaudily painted "adult" movie theater, but from 1948 to 1960 it was the site of the Dance Theater built by Lester Horton and a small group of dedicated co-workers on a shoestring and a dream. The building was miniscule in size, wedged between a flashy bar and a repair shop. To the casual passerby it was an unimpressive structure, but the bold colors of the building attested to the audacity of the undertaking. Whatever its physical shortcomings, and there were many, it held an undefinable fascination for many who walked by and for nearly all of us who walked through the famous double doors. It was a unique experiment—one that sometimes failed miserably, sometimes succeeded triumphantly. It launched many careers, changed many lives, and doubtless cost Horton his own.

To those of us who had the pleasure of visiting it in the late forties and early fifties, Dance Theater remains a magical memory, although I'm not sure that most of us realized the uniqueness of what we were seeing there any more than the critics did. Attendance at Horton's theater was not considered *de rigueur* for U.C.L.A. dance students at the time. Horton was too much of a maverick for our teachers, and we were hard at work at the time as disciples of Holm, Graham, and Humphrey. A few of us regularly attended events there anyway, for the dancers were excellent (and beautiful) and Horton was always trying out new ideas. In our infinite nineteen-year-old wisdom we would spend hours after the performances criticizing the works, sometimes scoffing mercilessly at some of the colorful, sexy dances and other times wishing we could borrow ideas from his serious pieces for our own student works.

      Like so many others at the time, we took Horton and his marvelous little theater for granted. It never occurred to us that the tall, heavy-set man with the worn face and twinkling eyes who sometimes stood at the door of his theater to greet the audience was one of the creative giants of twentieth-century dance.

acknowledgments

Elizabeth Talbot-Martin first brought the early Horton years in California to life for me. Toni Masarachia, Karoun Tootikian, Katherine Stubergh Keller, and Elsie Martinez spent long hours digging into the past. For the middle years, I am indebted to Dorathi Bock Pierre, Saida Gerrard, Bella Lewitzky, Newell Reynolds, Jeri Faubion Salkin, and James Mitchell. Anita Grossman, Rudi Gernreich, Herman Boden, Connie Finch Spriestersbach, Joyce Trisler, Carmen de Lavallade, James Truitte, and Constantine Hassalevris helped me to understand the spirit of Dance Theater. Without the help of William and Portia Bowne and Frank Eng, the work would not have been possible.

Thanks also to Robert M. Brown and Jon Boone for advice extended and to James K. Folsom for his help with the manuscript. Ronald Madison provided invaluable help in the early stages of this work, and Bette Johnson and Laura Wilber have been with it for a long time.

My appreciation to Bella Lewitzky, Joyce Trisler, Stanley Haggart, James Mitchell, James Truitte and Frank Eng (Dance Theater Collection) for lending me photos from their collections. Toyo Miyatake, Charles Van Mannen, Leo Salkin and Constantine Hassalevris graciously gave permission to use their outstanding work in this book. Wayloon Chuang faithfully reproduced the Horton sketches for *Salome* costumes from the originals.

xiii

My deep appreciation to Selma Jeanne Cohen who first printed portions of this writing in *Dance Perspectives No. 31,* to John Martin for saying, "I think there is a book here" long before there was, and to my wife Anne. . . .

The luxury of time to work on the writing was provided by a research award from the University of Wisconsin Graduate School in 1970, and help to complete the work came from a Research Board Grant from the University of Maryland in 1975.

Larry Warren
University Park, Maryland

illustrations

Lester Horton circa 1951   Frontispiece

Prairie Chicken Dance, 1929; *Pueblo Eagle Dance,* 1929;
     Lester Horton   28

Salome, 1934; Bruce Burroughs, Joy Montaya, Elizabeth
     Talbot-Martin; *Flight From Realty,* 1937; Lester Horton   77

Sacre du Printemps, Rehearsal, 1937; Bella Lewitzky;
     Renaldo Alarcon   78

Horton and group in idea session, 1941; Production
     preparations, 1941   99

Bella Lewitzky, James Mitchell, 1942   100

Dance Theater, 1950   127

Salome, 1948; Bella Lewitzky   129

The Park, 1949; Bella Lewitzky, Carl Ratcliff; *Totem
     Incantation,* 1948; Rudi Gernreich, Carl Ratcliff,
     Erik Johns   130

A Touch of Klee and Delightful 2, 1949; Rudi Gernreich,
     Carl Ratcliff, Louisa Kreck, Connie Finch   131

Soldadera, 1950; Bella Lewitzky   132

Warsaw Ghetto, 1949; Bella Lewitzky   133

Salome, 1950; James Truitte, Elle Johnson, Carmen de
     Lavallade; Workshop group, 1951   158

Lester Horton, 1952   159

Salome, Costume sketches, 1950   160-161

Another Touch of Klee, 1951; Carmen de Lavallade, James
     Truitte, Lelia Goldoni; Duke Ellington at Dance Theater,
     1951   162

Liberian Suite, Rehearsal, 1952; Alvin Ailey, Carmen de Lavallade
    in foreground   163
Liberian Suite, 1952; Henry Dunn, Norman Cornick and chorus;
    Joyce Trisler, James Truitte, Carmen de Lavallade   164
Lester Horton, 1952   177
Prado de Pena, 1952; Norman Cornick, Joyce Trisler, Richard
    D'Arcy, Carmen de Lavallade; Henry Dunn, Norman
    Cornick and chorus   178
Prado de Pena, 1952; Carmen de Lavallade, Norman Cornick   179
Lester Horton, Lelia Goldoni, 1952   180

lester
horton

the life and work

a regional theater is born

The 1904 marriage of Annie Lauders, 27, to Iredell Horton, 21, in Indianapolis, Indiana climaxed a scandal. Annie had been married to a farmer who lived on the outskirts of Peru, Indiana when she fell in love with the farm hand, Iredell. They ran off together, taking Annie's seven year old daughter, Hazel. It is unclear if there were any other children from her first marriage.* If so, they remained with their father. How Annie arranged for a divorce, what she did until it was legal, and how she came to have custody of the little girl are not known. It was a daring thing to have done in that place and at that time, but Annie had a strong will, and while she was not overly imaginative, neither was she troubled too much by convention.

At the time of her marriage she had a moderately pretty face, beautiful skin, and splendid hair which was her only vanity. A birdlike woman, determined and alert, Poly Anna knew her limitations but did not trouble about them. Her main concerns were to make her second marriage work and, when Lester Iradell [sic] was born on January 23, 1906, to care for her son.

In one or two interviews Lester Horton, who enjoyed indulging his fantasy on such occasions, told of a full-blooded

---

* Frank Eng believes that there were more sisters and/or brothers. Marion County, Indiana records shed no light and Horton's half sister, Mrs. Robert Painter, died before we were able to locate her.

3

Algonquin Indian grandmother. He also spoke from time to time of an abolitionist ancestor who had worked with the underground railroad helping slaves to the North and to freedom. Probably closest to the truth was his description of his forebears as a motley collection of English, Irish, and German immigrants who had settled in the Indianapolis area without particularly distinguishing themselves. His mother showed some originality in the variety of first names she used on legal documents. She chose between Poly Ann (marriage certificate), Annie (Lester's birth certificate), and Anna (census) apparently on whim. Lester liked his invention, Poly Anna, best.

Between the years 1904 and 1943, Iredell Horton worked variously as a laborer, stoker, custodian, and park attendant. Although he could be industrious, inventive, and even ingenious in working out the problems involved in repair and maintenance, Iredell drank just enough to keep his work from bringing in more than barely adequate funds to support his family, and Poly Anna soon became aware of her husband's inability to keep any but the most menial job.

The family moved often, four times by the time Lester was five years old. The fourth move was 60 miles southwest to the farm area of Brazil, Indiana, near Terre Haute. Here there were friends and some family upon whom Poly Anna could depend for moral and, if necessary, financial support. The move had also been prompted by the feeling that the good country air and way of life would be better for the youngsters than the near-slums of southwestern Indianapolis. And, quite simply, in the country the family could survive better on the meager income of an undependable laborer. Iredell worked when and as he could.

In his later years, Lester often spoke of the southern Indiana landscape and of its effect on his work. The fertile lower Wabash Valley was tranquil with the kind of lush countryside that inspired a group of idealists to build the Utopian community of New Harmony in the early nineteenth century. The seasons came and went gracefully, and there was time to watch small things happen.

Here Lester came to know more of the Hoosiers, the solid Indiana citizens who were typically prudent and practical—virtues he admired and sought in his friends but which he never developed himself. His more or less ordinary childhood was enhanced by the natural beauty of the place, and later he was to speak of his early childhood in a tone alive with remembered happiness. These early years were a continuous voyage of discovery, and he was forever bringing home relics from nature to an adoring mother and a sensitive, loving sister. Once, Poly Anna recalled, he commandeered the space between the windows and screens and proudly showed his family how Monarch butterflies are hatched from cocoons.

Though sometimes an overly emotional child, Lester was most often a bright, cheerful, and well-behaved boy, earning mostly A's in school, a child who liked to be liked and who worked hard for approval and affection. He became, in fact, an accomplished charmer. As one of his childhood friends later said, "He had this strange ability to take you along with his feelings. If Lester was enthusiastic about a project, it was a kind of magnetism—we'd all get excited about it, too. If something wasn't going well for him, we would be down in the dumps until he pulled out of it. He was a kind of Pied Piper." Lester was learning a great deal about how to win people. But his doting family was overprotective, and he was learning less than he would need to know about dealing with anger, both his own and that of others. It was not uncommon for him to run from stressful situations.

After World War I, Poly Anna and Iredell decided to try the city again. The Indianapolis to which the Hortons returned

in 1918 was a rapidly expanding industrial city, bustling with
activity, colorful, and proud of its past. This past had much to
excite an imaginative twelve-year-old boy. General Lew Wallace,
the Civil War hero and author who had written *Ben Hur* at his desk
in Crawfordsville, 45 miles away, had been an Indiana celebrity;
other Civil War veterans vividly recalled great battles, and everyone
was proud of having once had Abraham Lincoln as a neighbor.
Some folks traded stories their grandparents had told them, stories
of the great Indian tribes which had inhabited the Indiana territory,
tales of French explorers, fur traders, and missionaries who had
filtered into the area during the late seventeenth and early
eighteenth centuries. There were still Indians in the area who had
not yet relinquished their customs and way of life and who were
given a considerable amount of attention, for Indians were *culture*,
and there had been a drive for *culture* in Indianapolis since long
before the turn of the century.

   The Hortons eventually moved back to their old neighborhood and re-established their old pattern of life, with a few minor
improvements. In time, Iredell became something of a machinist,
but the family continued to live in a shabby part of the city.
Living in Indianapolis again was tremendously exciting for Lester.
He joined the library's Nature Study Group, and a new world of
landscapes opened up to him. One of his first excursions was to
the mysterious Indian mounds near Anderson, built by the first
known inhabitants of the area, a vanished people who are
referred to only as the Mound Builders. There was some specula-
tion at the time as to whether the mounds had served as a setting
for some forgotten ceremonial rite or as a place of burial. The
youngster was fascinated by these unanswered questions and began
to haunt the Children's Museum on Meridian Street, which had
exhibits relating to natural history, science, foreign cultures, and—
most important for Lester—splendid displays of American Indian
arts and artifacts. His interest in Indians practically became an

obsession. He was particularly fascinated by the Delaware, Miami, and Potawatomi tribes that had postdated the Mound Builders in the area.

The Children's Museum became his second home. He enrolled in craft classes, went on nature hikes, and attended story hours. Field trips to rustic and picturesque Brown County with its rolling forested hills were high spots in the young man's life. In 1950 he would title a work *Brown County, Indiana,* remembering that exceptionally beautiful place.

His parents wisely chose to trust their bright youngster in his choice of activities and, in general, to allow him a great deal of freedom to come and go as he needed. Lester's eighth-grade commencement program reveals that he was singled out for excellence in academic work, and as a special honor he was asked to read his composition, "The Indian in his Native Art." While sorting through his papers after his death, a close friend found the painstakingly handwritten paper Lester had carefully tucked away among his belongings.

At Shortridge High School he became fascinated by snakes, and whenever Horton's interest was stimulated, his aptitude for learning and memorizing increased dramatically. Surprisingly for one so sheltered in his early years he was not in the least bit squeamish. He enjoyed handling reptiles with an interest and familiarity that most people reserve for house pets and announced to his family that he was going to be a herpetologist, a specialist in that branch of zoology dealing with reptiles and amphibians. Temporarily at least, the snakes had won out over the Indians.

Lester was to change his mind when he saw the magnificent Denishawn Dancers (Ruth St. Denis, Ted Shawn, and company), touring at an early peak of their artistic powers. The program at the Murat Theatre featured Ted Shawn's Aztec ballet, *Xochitl,* as well as theatricalized dances inspired by the dance forms of India, Siam, Japan, Java, and Egypt. In addition to Shawn and

St. Denis, the cast included Charles Weidman, Doris Humphrey, and Martha Graham, who were, with Horton, to become the cornerstones of American modern dance. As he sat there in the gallery that December day in 1922, Horton found himself bewitched by the splendor of the costumes and by the sensuous, exotic movements of the dancers. An idea started to form in his mind: he knew he had to be part of that magic on the stage; he had to dance!

That was the story he told most frequently. In different versions he sometimes attributed his awakening to dance to a touring wild west show which featured American Indian dancing and, on other occasions, to a performance of Anna Pavlova and her company. Whichever version is the truth, we do know that in his early years he had a deep respect and admiration for Shawn and St. Denis, which he frequently expressed.

Whatever sent him there, it was Mlle. Theo Hewes to whom he went for his first lessons in dance. Mlle. Hewes had studied the Italian method on the East Coast with Madame Menzeli, the ballet teacher of society ladies, who had won fame in a production of *The Black Crook*. Mlle. Hewes had trained also in Chicago at the school of the Chicago Opera Company. Her studio advertisements announced her specialization in "toe dancing and ballet." Photos of the Theo Hewes dancers in recital reveal rampant eclecticism. One picture of Mlle. Hewes and partner in a dance entitled *The Sword* shows a gentleman, with sword held overhead, threatening a slight young girl in a kimono. The sword is easily five feet long, the kimono looks as though it were copied from an Oriental playing card, and Mlle. Hewes' expression is an odd combination of terror and repose. Another photo of her group shows three virginal youngsters in Greek costumes, posed in a turned-in *attitude* position, playing flutes with wild abandon.

In addition to the ballet work (he disliked the exacting physical discipline from the beginning) Horton took classes in aesthetic dance (Greek) and a very singular version of Denishawn. Though his body was not well designed for dance, he worked hard and made rapid strides at the school, and soon he was appearing in modest performances of the Theo Hewes Ballet, staged in its Indianapolis studio. Lester studied there for two years, becoming skilled enough to teach classes occasionally for Mlle. Hewes when she was indisposed. By the end of the second year the ballet mistress trusted him to handle Saturday classes at one of her other studios in Marion.

Talent of another kind was revealed at Shortridge High School, where Lester's work in art classes received special praise. Not only did his drawings show promise but, when he was introduced to the crafts of jewelry and pottery making, he was outstanding. His facility for and fascination with jewelry and its creation lasted throughout his lifetime and figured prominently in the costumes, props, and accessories he later designed. So appreciative was he of this early training that he later dedicated *Brown County, Indiana* to his inspiring high school art teacher, Rhoda Sellek.*

Soon dance engrossed him so completely that he could find time for only those school subjects which excited him, and he just as completely neglected the others. Finally he chose to drop out of high school. His family tried to dissuade him, but they were to discover that his beautiful head of hair was not the only thing he had inherited from his mother. He was at least as stubborn as she was.

Deciding to educate himself in his own way, he spent many hours at the public library, where he memorized Indian stories, songs, and chants, and carefully deciphered descriptions of Indian dances. Drama critic Walter Hickman, writing in the *Indianapolis Times* ten years later, recalled having personally observed "Horton's passionate studies of Indian Lore."

*The program spells it Roda Selleck, which is incorrect.

Another performance of the Denishawn Dancers which he saw at the Murat Theatre in 1923 fed the flames. This time the highlights were St. Denis' *Ishtar of the Seven Gates* and Shawn's own American Indian Dance, *The Feather of the Dawn.* That the latter work had a profound effect on Horton's early dance years is evidenced by his frequent mention of the piece during his own "Indian period" in Los Angeles. Later he sought out and worked with its composer, Homer Grunn.

The year 1925 marked Lester Horton's first modest personal contact with the professional world of dance. In that year, a Denishawn teacher and choreographer, Forrest Thornburg, who later established the Nashville Civic Ballet, came to Indianapolis to recruit dancers for a local presentation of a touring company featuring the violinist Mellie Dunham. A square dance number was to be included. Thornburg chose Lester as the outstanding male dancer at the audition and gave him his first professional job. The competition for the job was not very stiff. Everyone who showed up at the audition was hired.

A warm, easy friendship developed between the affable young dancer, the choreographer, and his bride-to-be, who came along on the trip. The Thornburgs remember the nineteen-year-old Lester as being witty, ingratiating, and hard working. Between rehearsals Thornburg taught Lester some Denishawn dances and Lester, in turn, aided the choreographer in rehearsals, proving to be an adept assistant. The experience was a stimulating and exciting one for Lester, who remembered the material for years afterward.

When Iredell, whose fortunes continued to decline, decided to move back to Brazil, Indiana once again, Lester made a decision of his own. He would stay in Indianapolis. Earning enough from various part-time jobs to be on his own, he was somehow able to scrape together the money for a few lessons from renowned ballet master Adolph Bolm in Chicago, 175 miles away. But this training period was not destined to last beyond lesson number two, for Bolm, who had startled Paris in 1909 with his magnificent dancing in the Diaghilev Ballet, was a strict taskmaster. Lester liked Russian ballet training no more than the Italian version he had resisted in Mlle. Hewes' studio. One final attempt in the mid-twenties to study ballet, this time at the Pavley-Oukrainsky School, also in Chicago, had similar results. Nevertheless, Horton remembered those old maestros fondly and always spoke highly of Bolm years later when both of them were teaching in Los Angeles. When he started teaching on his own some years later, the difficulty of his classes made the ones he avoided seem tame.

"Give us a theater" was the cry. "Give us a stage manager, one or two professional actors and some amateur students. Give us a few colored lights and a cheesecloth background. Give us a bandbox for a stage, and we can produce, and what is better, perpetuate, the finer dramas of the age. In fifty years we will have little theaters in every city of any size in the Union. We should have one in Indianapolis now." The seeds of the Indianapolis Little Theatre were planted in February, 1914, when Professor William E. Jenkins, Indiana University Librarian, made this plea in a lecture before the Indianapolis Center of the Drama League. From Boston to Los Angeles the little theater movement was underway. A folk theater was coming into being in the United States—a movement which gave to the motion pictures and the stage some of their brightest stars, finest plays, and most brilliant directors and choreographers.

One of the citizens to rise to Professor Jenkins' challenge was playwright William O. Bates, who was fond of describing himself as a "semi-reformed newspaperman whose work as a dramatic critic on the *Indianapolis Star* led to his downfall into playwriting." He had authored several plays which had been

performed in the Midwest, including *Uncle Rodney* (1896) and
Jacob Leisler (1913). At the first meeting of the Board of
Directors of the Little Theatre Society of Indiana, Mr. Bates was
elected Secretary, and he and his wife, Clara Nixon Bates, became
leading lights in the early development of the group. The Little
Theatre quickly evolved into a unique organization: while
basically conservative and middle class, it occasionally presented
such then-controversial plays as Pirandello's *Six Characters in
Search of an Author* and Capek's *R.U.R.* A critic complained
that the "Little Theatre discloses a naïve willingness to hold
aloft the cross of the morality play with one hand while it
dangles the lid of social garbage from the other." Undaunted,
the little group went on to produce a motley variety of plays
in the Sculpture Court of the John Herron Art Institute. Since
the group had no public funding and no patron, it was necessary
for members to participate in all phases of the theater's productions. It was not uncommon, for example, for an enthusiastic
performer to help out with costume construction in the hours
before rehearsal, paint props during the rehearsal itself, and
afterwards drive to the scenery shop several blocks away to work
on sets. On opening night the sets were loaded on a horse-
drawn wagon and delivered to the theater in time to do touch-up
work in case the open vehicle had encountered rain, hail, or snow
on its way. Without this kind of effort there could have been no
regional theater in America.

In the early 1920s William and Clara Bates attempted, with
some success, to interest the Little Theatre in producing the work
of amateur playwrights. Both had an ardent interest in developing
native talent and were particularly interested in Indiana history,
folkways, and the region's American Indian heritage. Mr. Bates
was a charter member of the Society of Colonial Wars and an
ardent collector of Indian relics. In 1920 he had written the script
for the Indiana Centennial pageant, and the project had been a

huge success. He also helped and encouraged young writers, especially if they wrote about indigenous subject matter. The couple plainly felt a responsibility to publicize still further their point of view. Mrs. Bates went so far as to sponsor a contest in which cash prizes were awarded for the best plays dealing with Hoosiers and their way of life (an "impartially selected" jury chose Mr. Bates to receive one of his wife's awards to every-one's apparent delight).* Although some of the winning plays were produced, the Little Theatre was headed in a different direction.

The gifted actor George Somnes, one of the stars of the Stuart Walker Stock Company which played part of each year in Indianapolis, was invited to become director of the group. It was his belief, and later Horton's, that the amateur theater is a myth and that any step in the realm of theater is a step toward pro-fessionalism and with this attitude, for two years he poured all he knew of stagecraft into his work with the Little Theatre. When he left, the group remained essentially unchanged in outlook, but its standards of performance and production had been raised considerably. The Bateses learned a great deal from the early Somnes period and, in order to realize some of their own ideas, they decided to apply themselves to a new enterprise—the for-mation of the Indianapolis Theatre Guild.

For this venture, they turned from the direction of the Little Theatre movement to the work of Frederick H. Koch, inspired advocate of folk drama and community pageants who had been involved in the renowned George Pierce Baker work-shop at Harvard. After graduation in 1906, fired with enthu-siasm generated by the famous Baker, he formed a small com-pany which performed Sheridan's *The Rivals* in six prairie towns in North Dakota. To give some indication of the Yankee zeal of this ingenious little group, it is worth remarking that they would court their new and somewhat startled potential audiences

---

*Little Theatre Society of Indiana, *Indiana Prize Plays*, preface by William O. Bates (Indianapolis, Indiana: Bobbs-Merril, 1924).

by distributing handbills in full period costume. After a few years
of this grassroots pioneering, Koch became interested in pageantry
and, with his considerable enthusiasm now focused in this direction, he accepted a teaching position at the University of North
Dakota. Under Koch's guidance, graduate students went out into
rural communities, even as far west as Montana, to stir up more
pageant making. In many cases, members of the community
were involved in the writing of the scenario, and sometimes
hundreds participated in the performances.* The Indianapolis
Theatre Guild was to work towards this kind of rich communal
effort, and Lester Horton would be a central figure in the work.

Just as the Bateses were considering their initial production, William Bates succumbed to a heart attack. After a suitable
period of mourning, Mrs. Bates got busy. She would carry on the
project alone.

It is a remarkable coincidence if Clara Nixon Bates did not
read Ted Shawn's delightful 1926 book, *The American Ballet,*†
for in it he suggests doing a pageant based on Longfellow's poem,
The Song of Hiawatha, and this is exactly what she did. A play
on the theme by Olive M. Price was the launching point from
which, with additional themes and characters from the famous
poem, Mrs. Bates created an outline for a music, drama, and
dance pageant.

Her ideas were well thought out. Indian dances had been
shown on the banks of the canal in Indianapolis' Fairview Park
the previous summer. Why not use that as the site for the production? It could be an annual community project, done out-
of-doors every year. She had learned a great deal about production, promotion, and fund raising during her years as an
active Little Theatre member. She had heard of a gifted young
man at the Theo Hewes School, had seen him, as a matter of
fact, at the Little Theater Costume Ball a few months earlier

*Kenneth Macgowan, *Footlights Across America* (New York: Harcourt, Brace, 1929)
†Ted Shawn, *The American Ballet* (New York: Henry Holt, 1926).

in an outrageously funny satirical drag costume he had designed. The costume had won a prize against some very strong competition. Lester received a note inviting him to have tea with Clara Bates at her home in Woodruff Place.

Beautiful Woodruff Place! Showcase of the affluent. Lester loved to bicycle through the residential park when he was a boy, drawn by esplanades of velvety grass, flower beds, fountains, stone urns, statuary, and an ornate gate house. The homes were large and lavishly ornamented with gingerbread cupolas, trellised vines, and stained-glass windows. T.C. Steele, Indiana's most famous artist, lived there, as did the author of *Seventeen*, Booth Tarkington. The stately Bates home stood on a corner adjacent to one of the elaborate fountains. The nineteen-year-old dancer thought that he would be happy to be living in the carriage house. Six months later, he was.

The interview went well. After being introduced to Clara Bates' Persian cats, Lester was shown into a room housing a fine collection of Indian drums, rattles, blankets, pottery, and jewelry. He spoke thoughtfully and intelligently about each item as he looked about, touching things he had only read about before or seen in the museum. He also liked Clara Bates' ideas for *The Song of Hiawatha*, and soon he was adding some of his own. He agreed to work with her on the project.

Arrangements were made for several trips to Indiana reservations so that Lester could study at first hand the dances he would be performing and teaching for *Hiawatha*. The following spring he spent several weeks in Santa Fe where, through some of William Bates' business and professional connections, Lester was given the opportunity to learn from excellent Indian performers who taught him dances as well as complex chants. He claimed to have been invited to perform in public with his teachers; a rare compliment if true. The costumes and accessories he sketched while in Santa Fe were later reproduced in large quantities for the pageant.

Once back in Indianapolis, Clara Bates got the Indianapolis Theatre Guild into full swing, recruiting dancers, musicians,
and helpers of all kinds, together with the lifeblood of such
ambitious undertakings, sponsors. After he was named Art
Director and Dance Master and was given the title role, Lester
was sent to the Field Museum in Chicago for more design
research. The young art director then set up a workshop where
he could teach his "staff" the necessary skills for making re-
productions of Indian clothing and accessories. Here he had his
first experience exploring the potential of inexpensive fabrics to
substitute for the real thing. He found that white flannel, dyed
light brown and hand painted, looked like bead-encrusted leather
at ten paces, that tie-dyeing was splendid for special effects, and
that mixing poster paints with soap made them last longer. The
results were excellent.

The production was mounted on the shores of the canal
passing through Fairview Park. Indian tepees were erected and
bonfires were built for performances. The audiences sat on the
opposite side of the canal to view the action. A forty-piece
community orchestra played "authentic" Indian melodies
throughout the performance, including everything from
orchestrated native Indian chants to the "Largo" from Dvořák's
New World Symphony. Jewelry and blankets from the Bates
collection were used in the performance which was seen by
approximately 500 people.

An enthusiastic viewer wrote:

> One of the most impressive scenes was that of the death of
> the Indian Girl followed by the departure of Hiawatha to
> the "Promised Land." Just as the sun dropped behind the
> trees, the sorrowing youth removed all his beads of tribal
> distinction and in a canoe glided down the water, softly
> singing his note of farewell.

A year later during the same scene, the canoe broke loose from
its invisible wire, and Clara Bates had to call the fire department
to rescue Lester, who had drifted a considerable distance toward
the "Happy Hunting Ground."

  The production was a triumph both for Clara Bates and
for Horton. Her years of work for the Little Theatre and her
close association with the production of the Indiana Centennial
Pageant had paid off handsomely. Lester's contribution had
been considerable, for in addition to supervising the construction
of sets, costumes, and accessories, he had taught several dances to
the cast and, according to the reviews, had a considerable personal
success as a performer. He was twenty years old and was learning
a great deal. Part of his success in the venture came from his
ability to carry people away with his own enthusiasm. He somehow believed that others were as excited as he was about a
given undertaking, and his believing it often made it so.

  Clara Bates was able to arrange additional performance
dates, and in the next year *The Song of Hiawatha* was presented
throughout Indiana and in major cities in Ohio as well. The
procedure was always the same. Some prominent ladies in the
community were contacted and invited to be sponsors "in the
interests of education and culture for the young people of
America, that they may be more fully acquainted with the
history and the ideal customs of the American Indian." Calls
went out for dancers, actors, and singers. By the time the
permanent cast arrived, Mrs. Bates and Lester had been there for
some time making preparations. Their role was actually very
similar to the "advance men" of the touring circuits. Large
audiences for the performances were assured by the numerous
enthusiastic sponsors. A low admission was charged, and
orphanages were usually admitted free. It was colorful and
novel, appealing to the intellectuals as well as the less educated.
The Midwesterner of the 1920s was still fascinated by the former
inhabitants of the land.

Clara Bates had been quite impressed by the samples she had seen of Lester's art work and, convinced that she had uncovered a brilliant young artist, in the autumn of 1926 offered to pay his tuition at the fine John Herron Art Institute in Indianapolis. She was not a wealthy woman, but she was taken with this gifted and ingratiating young man. Years before, her husband had helped some promising young writers, and it was good to continue his work. Her motive was, of course, partially selfish. Since he was in her debt, Lester would have to stay with *Hiawatha* through at least one more season.

Several months later she noticed that Lester was looking overworked and underfed. It was obvious that he was neglecting himself to a point where he was impairing his health. Also, she was becoming impatient when he was not available to join her for early morning or late night production discussions. She suggested that he come to live in her attractive small carriage house where she could keep an eye on him and see that he ate properly. He accepted her hospitality but wisely kept his own tiny apartment to avoid an overdose of tender loving care. He was given a set of keys to the big house.

New York and Chicago Bohemianism had filtered through to the limited art world of Indianapolis by the mid-twenties and the Herron Institute was an extremely lively place. There was a fine faculty, and the institution had a healthy touring exhibit policy. Students were exposed to the best in American and European art. Nonconformity was the order of the day, and the young artist-dancer fit in admirably. Students dressed eccentrically. Lester let his hair grow long. There was much discussion about reincarnation; Lester became interested in theosophy; he attended séances. His interest in the unusual and bizarre had been sparked by the study of Indian cult practices, and he was quite ready to accept the probability, suggested by sculptress Myra Richards, that he had been of royal blood in a previous incarnation. This suggestion may have been prompted by the fact that Lester had once again triumphed in high society by winning the prize for the most original costume at the 1927 Little Theatre "Arabian Nights Ball." His costume was described as "strikingly beautiful . . . gold cloth of a Chinese Prince." Throughout his life Lester preferred beautiful fabric to groceries and, with his meager income, he often had to make a choice between the two.

When Clara Bates was not at home, Lester sometimes invited friends to participate in séances in her ornately furnished living room. It was even rumored that in her absence voodoo rituals and peyote smoking had taken place behind those handsome Victorian doors, but his benefactress chose to ignore the talk. If any scandal had openly erupted, the Horton story would surely have taken a different turn.

The 1927 production of *The Song of Hiawatha* was enlivened by the presence of Blair Taylor, nephew of General Lew Wallace and University of Michigan graduate. A vivacious and intelligent bachelor, Taylor seemed to have had several consuming interests: making money, studying ancient and recent Indian history, collecting rare books, and, of course, the theater. At the age of 26 he had gone off to manage a huge sugar plantation in Cuba. By 1927, he was back in Indianapolis with a large black Buick, a good deal of money, and a desire to pursue his other interests in the leisure time that affluence allowed. For a while he adopted Lester, and together they hunted pottery shards in the Burial Mounds or went off in search of Indians who might be willing to sell a treasured trinket. They often made trips to Crawfordsville, where Taylor was taking an active part in the restoration of the house in which his uncle had written *Ben Hur*.

During the 1927 production and subsequent tours of *The Song of Hiawatha*, Taylor was around a great deal, footing bills and paying small attentions to the company. At one performance he showed up with several bottles of bootleg liquor, and one of the older actresses, who was supposed to run out of a tepee and interrupt Lester's "Invocation to the Thunder God," staggered out in a drunken stupor and fell at Hiawatha's feet, smiling happily. The young warrior kept invoking over the apparently lifeless body until the stage manager finally read her lines and carried her offstage. Lester enjoyed the incident and proceeded to create an amusing imitation of the unique performance.

After almost a year of work at the Herron Institute, Horton felt the need to try his own artistic wings and to get away from Clara Bates' watchful eye. He moved to Chicago where, for a while, he supported himself by washing dishes. Later he got a job with a large Chicago costume house, where he added to his understanding of the basics of costume design and construction and learned how to draw costume plates—a skill he was later to use extensively. Combining ideas from Hewes, Denishawn, and his own authentic materials, he began creating Oriental and American Indian dances, theatricalized by his design and theater training. He later recalled having performed these solo dances in "a little theater of the avante-garde art colony of Chicago's North Side," but the income from this work was negligible.

While prohibition and mob warfare were making the headlines, less touted but no less exciting things were happening in theater and the arts in Chicago, where the impact of modernism was at an early peak. The influential *Little Review* and *Poetry Magazine* were flourishing, and the radical theater movement was attracting attention. Horton was on the periphery of the scene, befriending artists, writers, and dancers who were involved in these experimental activities.

young man
goes west

Clara Nixon Bates was not about to let *The Song of Hiawatha* go by the board. She contacted an old California friend, socialite Lysbeth Argus of Eagle Rock, about the production. The Argus family had a natural amphitheater on their estate which had been transformed into a modest outdoor theater, the "Argus Bowl." Music, theater, and dance events were presented there for the enjoyment of people living in that remote part of Los Angeles between Glendale and Pasadena. Mrs. Argus was so enthusiastic about *Hiawatha* that she offered to help bring the worthwhile educational project to California, to recruit the necessary actors, dancers, and musicians—and, most importantly, to find patrons for the production.

Lester was wary at first about accepting Clara Bates' summons to hear of the new plan, for he had been feeling increasingly pressured by her apparent desire to tie him to that production forever. On the other hand, Chicago had not "discovered" him, and he hated living in the city. The prospect of spending some time in the far West was actually as intriguing to him as the possibility of professional opportunities in California. He remembered reading that Ted Shawn had once owned a small house in Eagle Rock, California. That was a good omen. He accepted because he knew he had little to lose.

21

Lester was pleased by the choice of Donella Donaldson
for the part of Minnehaha. Donella was a talented and wistfully
beautiful young blond who would one day, with the stage name
Julie Haydon, win fame as Laura in the original production of
Tennessee Williams' *Glass Menagerie* and would later marry the
famed theater critic, George Jean Nathan. On the date set for
the departure tin trunks laden with costumes, feathers, headdresses, and assorted homemade and authentic American Indian
percussion instruments were tied to the roof of Clara Bates'
touring sedan. That formidable lady must have had the determined look of a general about to enter combat as she drove past
her curious Woodruff Place neighbors with her precious cargo of
trinkets and talent. She was, after all, on a cultural mission!
The little troupe headed west for the California debut of *The
Song of Hiawatha* and Lester Horton.

The arrival of Clara Bates and company was duly noted
in the society column of the *Los Angeles Times.* Lysbeth Argus
had done her work well. Dozens of sponsors had been enlisted.
Among those were the composer Charles Wakefield Cadman
("From the Land of the Sky Blue Water") and composer-writer
Carrie Jacobs Bond ("I Love You, Truly"). The cast was
impressed by the magnetic young director, and they worked
well for him. By this time, he was expert at transforming
ordinary folks into immortal Indians, and opening night, July 2,
1928, was another personal triumph for Lester. He even had a
few *real* Indians in this production. Some local Indian experts
declared the work to be authentic, and from then on Lester was
treated as an important artist both by his young cast and by the
older people who had come to support the venture. The highly
respected Mr. Cadman was quoted as saying, "I regard Mr. Horton
as one of America's most original creative artists." Plans were
launched for a west coast tour of *Song of Hiawatha*, and Lester
was invited to live in a converted chicken house on the Argus
Estate. He was completely taken with Southern California and

spent long hours familiarizing himself with the large variety of
plants, birds, and other wildlife which were part of the new
landscape.

One of the dancers who had been chosen for the cast of
Hiawatha was Katherine Stubergh, a ballet student whose family
was in the business of making wax figures. She and Horton
immediately became fast friends, having in common a deep love
of dance and a droll sense of humor. Katherine's warm, loving
"Mama" approved the friendship, and it was not long before the
Stuberghs began treating Lester as one of the family.

The Stuberghs, now world-famous for their lifelike
figures of theater celebrities and historical figures, invited Lester
to see their studio and, when they became familiar with his
skills, offered him employment as needed. This was to be the
most enduring friendship of his lifetime. " 'Mama' came religiously to each performance of *Hiawatha* and, after one, came
up to Lester, whispering to him that when the wind blew against
his loincloth, 'you could see white skin.' 'Don't worry, Mama,'
Horton reassured her, 'it's all absolutely authentic.' " Another
dancer in the production recalled that, after one particularly
stirring performance of the "Invocation to the Thunder God,"
the audience was startled to hear a crash of thunder in the starry
California night, followed by a few drops of rain, which was
almost unheard of in that part of the country in July.

The production of *Hiawatha* has been variously described
by critics as "the passion play of America," "very pretty," and
"not really very much of anything—dull, as a matter of fact."
The last comment came from Jean Abel, a Glendale High School
teacher who in a few years would give Horton his first chance
to develop some of his own creative work. When the production
reached San Francisco, Redfern Mason was impressed, "The
words were Longfellow's; . . . the music is tribal from coast
to coast; the dances and ceremonies are authentic . . . it was
like slipping away from this workaday world into that folk life

which is the primitive poetry of America." The press was exceptionally complimentary to Horton for his portrayal of Hiawatha. Some twenty-five performances were given in California during the next few years, and excerpts and revisions of the material were to remain in Horton's repertory for some time to come.

Midway through the tour that summer the relationship between Clara Bates and her young star began to show signs of strain. She objected when he wandered off on his own as he often did, forgetting to leave word of where he was going or when he would be coming back. She worried constantly about funds and was annoyed with him when he spent his tiny allowance on trinkets or books, missing meals to do so. He wanted to try a few new ideas; she wanted to stay in the *Hiawatha* business forever, or so it seemed to him. She questioned his gratitude, and he felt used. Finally it was decided that she would return to Indianapolis without him. He promised one more production of *Hiawatha* the following summer. It was not that he did not appreciate what she had done for him; he had simply outgrown her.

During the summer tour Ivor Boroloff, a young man who wished desperately to become an actor, attached himself to Lester, who was at first flattered by the attention. His ambitious mother proposed a partnership in which Horton would provide acting lessons and theater know-how. She would take care of business matters, and with a bit of her own money and earnings from their performances they would open a studio in Oakland, across the bay from San Francisco. This city was extremely responsive to the *Hiawatha* production. An elaborate organization had been developed to support performances there, and the young director's skill in handling nonprofessional community casts did not go unnoticed. Letters of endorsement for the proposed school, "where our good literature can come

to life in music, drama and pageantry" were sent out by numer-
ous patrons, including society people and professors at the
University of California. Seeking performances in the San
Francisco area, the two young men signed with an agent.
The publicity announced:

Ivor Boroloff
Diseur and Mime
and
Lester Horton
(Okoya Tihua)
In A Cycle Of
Authentic and Dramatic Dances
New on the Pacific Coast
Dance Material May Be Adapted
For All Occasions

Horton's professional name for a short time, Okoya Tihua, was
from American Indian mythology.

There being no great demand for a program combining
elocution, mime, and American Indian dancing, the attraction
was not successful. Prospects for the new school did not look
good, and the young actor and his mother were making matters
worse by trying to domesticate Lester, much as Clara Bates had
tried to do.

In the autumn of 1928, while cutting down saplings to
use as props for *Hiawatha* in a eucalyptus grove in Piedmont,
California, Horton met Elsie Martinez, her daughter Michaela,
and Harriet Dean. The ladies introduced themselves and soon
found that they had much in common with Lester. Miss Dean
was from Indianapolis and had spent several years in Chicago as
a fund raiser for the *Little Review*. Elsie Martinez' Mexican-
born husband, Xavier, was a fine artist, an intimate of Rivera

and Orozco. Her father, the journalist Herman Whittaker, had
helped to expose a slave market in Mexico, gone on two
campaigns with Pancho Villa and, during World War I, been chosen
by William Randolph Hearst to "explain America and England
to each other." Michaela was going to become an artist like
her father. Horton was invited to dinner and told his story.
Forty-five years later, "Pellie" Martinez remembered:

> He had a large variety of interests and was very receptive.
> We were very interested in the Indians of the Southwest
> and he knew a great deal . . . had a feel for the people.
> He was overtired, emotionally strained, and smoked too
> much. He invited us to the *Hiawatha* thing and it was
> good. He had remarkable talent. We had a feeling he
> wouldn't last long and got busy. A few visits later he
> was invited to stay with us for as long as he needed to.
> The first step was to get rid of these people who were
> draining him. It was not kind, but it had to be done.
> He lived in the little room we called the crow's nest, or
> artist's corner. (The bathroom walls were signed by
> writers George Sterling, Robert Service, and Jack London.
> They were dubbed "Knights of the Bath.") His only
> responsibility was to rest and think about what he would
> like to do with his future. He wanted to do something
> beyond the commonplace. That would take time. At
> first we just wanted him to be free. He would spend
> hours in his room every day, thinking and drawing
> sketches. At night we'd get together, and he would tell
> us what he'd been working on. He knew he wanted to
> work in a more modern vein but didn't quite know
> where to start. Some evenings he would dance for us,
> or experiment with make-up. We had this nosy neighbor,
> who was in the habit of glaring through her front window
> to see what was going on at our house. Lester fixed her
> by devising the most gruesome, grisly make-up ever seen
> and scaring her half to death.

He could have us in stitches doing impressions of the
cultured ladies of Indianapolis. Pal [Harriet Dean] knew
many of them. Other nights we'd talk. We wanted to
bring his perceptiveness into a wider field and we didn't
have to work hard at it. Pal, fresh from the *Little Review,*
argued that the important thing was to be current. In
her way she was a bit of a radical. Once she had invited
Emma Goldman to speak to the Indianapolis society
ladies about free love . . . I fought for a deep understanding of the past. We'd have colossal uproars. We
introduced him to Spengler. Some nights we just
listened to wonderful music. My husband was a wild,
picturesque Mexican who was very fond of Lester and
nicknamed him Quaché, the Hopi word for buddy (pal).

He liked the Navajo shirt that Marty [Mr. Martinez] wore.
We made him one of his own, which he loved and wore
all the time. It was a fine time, having Lester with us
those three months. He had such a beautiful spirit.
Well, we had to get him going. San Francisco was not
the place to be at that time. The whole focus was
European culture. Los Angeles made better sense. For
better or worse, they are always ready to try something
new . . . The important thing is the release of what is
within you, don't you think?

In 1973 this matchless woman, still vibrant with life in
her eighties, had among her projects helping a young actor to
build an accurate impersonation of Jack London from her vivid
childhood recollections, and the preparation of oral history tapes
for the University of California, in which she described the San
Francisco area of her youth.

Horton's easy acceptance into this wonderful family of
artists was to be invaluable to him in his personal growth. In
1939 he wrote to them:

Prairie Chicken Dance, 1929;
Lester Horton.
(Photo by Toyo Miyatake.)

Pueblo Eagle Dance, 1929;
Lester Horton.
(Photo by Toyo Miyatake.)

> My memories go back to the long walks to the grove with
> Pellie's finger pointing downward and Pal's good-natured
> gait. The warm greetings when I would return from San
> Francisco and the odors from Pellie's kitchen . . . You
> may have fogotten all this, but it dwells in my mind
> constantly. You helped to make a decent human being
> out of me. I shall never forget it. I hope some day to
> develop a work which may satisfy you that all the time
> given me was not wasted.

After fulfilling his performance commitments in the San
Francisco area, Lester, with advice from his new friends, dis-
entangled himself from Boroloff and the Oakland project and
returned to Eagle Rock. Mrs. Argus, who had become quite
fond of him, welcomed him to stay on in the chicken house as
long as he liked.

Taking his cue from the bright California sunshine, he
painted the walls a light yellow. Indian blankets together with
feathered headdresses and a few masks hanging from the walls
stood out boldly, creating an impression of artistic opulence.
The house was comfortable in a makeshift, Spartan way, partly
out of preference but more out of financial necessity. For most
of Horton's life he lived in spaces which combined living and
working places in the same area.

In June, 1929, *American Dancer* magazine published an
article by Lester Horton, "American Indian Dancing." It is
well-written and informative:

> If dancers would only make an effort, to preserve this
> beauty which exists literally at our back doors, something
> magnificent might be born. A dance can be built upon
> these art forms that would be truly representative of this
> great country, something new and fundamental.

In describing some of the actual steps, he comes up with the startling
statement, "There are movements which approximate some used in

the *Charleston* and *Varsity Drag*, though it is doubtful if there is any
real connection between the two."

Katherine Stubergh fondly recalled:

> Lester read a great deal and appeared to retain everything
> but he could be one of the most delightful frauds, really,
> that you'd ever want to know. He could be terribly
> pompous. He held his big head very high, with his back
> as straight as a ramrod and he would make a positive
> statement, completely wrong, and just delight everyone.
> When he was being his most pompous, he was most
> delightful.

We will probably never know just how much of an expert
in American Indian Dance Horton was. It is certain that no other
non-Indian on the West Coast during the late 1920s and 1930s
matched his accomplishment in interesting people in this aspect
of our heritage.

In 1929 Michio Ito invited Horton to perform with his
company. The Japanese-born Ito, a former student of Emile
Jaques-Dalcroze, danced, choreographed, and taught in the
United States during the years between World War I and 1948.
Before settling in California he had performed and taught in New
York, where he had produced full evenings of dance, providing
an opportunity for new and valuable talents to perform in his
Pinwheel review. He was the choreographer of *The Garden of
Kama*, in which Martha Graham appeared in the 1923 Greenwich
Village Follies, and in 1930 he presented a series of Japanese
popular plays at the Booth Theater.

Ito's movement vocabulary was oriented toward the use
of the upper body: head, shoulders, and, most importantly, the
arms. The legs served primarily as a moving base to complete
the spatial pattern of the dance. He often choreographed to the
music of Schumann, Beethoven, Borodin, Scriabin, and Debussy.
For symphonic choreographies he sometimes employed more

than a hundred dancers. As part of his California repertory, Ito
produced William Butler Yeats' plays for dancers, and in at least
one of these, *At The Hawk's Well,* Horton played a leading role.
From Ito, Horton learned what he called the "organic use of
props," which was to figure so prominently in his work; and the
seed of his concept of the "choreodrama" possibly evolved from
his experience with plays for dancers. From all accounts Ito's
modernism had strong roots in Japanese theater forms.

As a performer, Ito had an enormous personal dynamic.
Horton was able to observe and study the stage projection of
a competent artist who could command the attention and interest
of his audience by the stateliness of his bearing and the clarity
and forcefulness of his projection of gesture. His body spoke
eloquently; his facial expression was calm, mask-like. These
performance skills were integrated into Horton's understanding
of theater dance and later he was able to refine them and pass
them along to his dancers. Bella Lewitzky, Carmen de Lavallade,
Lelia Goldoni, and Joyce Trisler were only a few of the Horton-
trained dancers who could perform with the authority of
seasoned artists while still in their teens.

The Song of Hiawatha was given six performances in June
of 1929 with Lester Horton directing. Mrs. Bates was back as
chairman of the endeavor to assist her former protégé in the
final productions of her beloved work. This time, in addition
to Charles Wakefield Cadman, Sol Cohen and Homer Grunn
helped with the music. Over 225 "Hostesses" were listed. After
overseeing the Eagle Rock performances and a short tour, Mrs.
Bates returned to Indianapolis to continue to work on modest
productions of the Theatre Guild and arrange cat shows at the
Indiana State Fairground. She had been pleased with Lester's
success but never quite forgave him for deserting *The Song of
Hiawatha* when it was doing so well.

Occasional performances of his solo repertory were
providing a very meager income and Horton was not

eating properly. Tinned sardines were his staple. Once again he
was impairing his health, possibly permanently this time.
Katherine Stubergh recalled:

> In the early 1930s he was chosen to play the Indian fire
> god in a pageant they used to put on in Palm Springs.
> He designed a costume covered with diamond-shaped
> sequins, graduated in color. It was really quite spec-
> tacular, and in later years we had a good laugh over it.
> After the performance, when Lester didn't appear, Mama
> and I became concerned and went to look for him. We
> found him, nearly unconscious, on the floor of his
> dressing room. I believe he'd had a mild heart attack.
> We took him to live with us in a cottage we rented near
> his place in Eagle Rock. He was very ill for a long time.
> When he recovered we convinced him to come and work
> for us.

At the Stubergh's wax studio one of Horton's jobs was
to paint faces on store window mannequins. His great facility
with paints and theatrical make-up made him valuable in this
work which would provide sustenance, off and on, for some
years to come. Often, too, a few years later, one or another of
Horton's dancers would be given temporary employment at the
studio. The Stuberghs undoubtedly had the only workshop in
the city where employees tapped Indian rhythms and chanted
tribal songs while they worked.

By 1931, Horton's creative drive seemed to be temporarily
on the wane. Perhaps the comfort of life in the chicken house
and a steady income from the Stuberghs made him less ambitious.
The magnificence of the scenery, the great, open sky with purple
hued mountains, the endless expanse of the Pacific with the
desert only an hour or two away have inspired many, but far
more have been seduced by the beauty and almost vulgar ease
of life. For someone of Horton's temperament the temptation

was particularly great. People who can fantasize can wait. There
is no need for immediate solutions to problems, artistic or otherwise.

In his free time Lester went to museums, libraries, exhibits, wandering wherever his insatiable, childlike curiosity led him.
He was trying to discover the future direction for his life, looking
for some possibilities for his development as an artist. In mocca-
sins, baggy corduroy pants, Navajo shirt, Indian jewelry, and
bushy, longish hair he must have admirably suited the role of
the young artist. Forty years later he might have been lost among
the thousands who had "gone Indian." In his own way he was
busy unconsciously, perhaps, gaining strength for what lay ahead.
Again, Katherine Stubergh tells us:

> Lester was always digging things up and bringing them in
> to show us. He made me handle a snake. I was very
> squeamish. He got me over that; there was no choice.
> He never took anything [in nature] for granted and his
> awe taught me how to look at things. It could be a cold,
> gloomy day . . . he would turn over a large rock and we
> would see some life, some design. He would find beauty.

Elsie Martinez and Harriet Dean got the message. Lester
was now well, after the long illness, but was not making very
great strides down there in the South. They suggested that he
call on a friend of theirs, Jean Abel, the Glendale High School
art teacher. Jean Abel, a woman of great vitality and imagination, invited Lester to direct and choreograph an Indian pageant
at the high school, using art and drama students. Under his
guidance, the eager teen-agers learned to perform a large variety
of American Indian dances with some degree of style and polish.
During art classes and after school they worked on their own props,
costumes, and musical instruments. The costumes were excellent,
and Lester created exciting lighting effects. Abel, who had seen

and not cared for *The Song of Hiawatha,* recognized the young dancer's outstanding ability to create extraordinarily attractive stage patterns with inexperienced youngsters who seemed to love every minute of the work. Lester, it seemed, was a born teacher.

By all accounts an inspired and inspiring teacher herself, Jean Abel recognized an extraordinary talent. She was impressed, too, by Lester's erudition. "I can scarcely remember," she said, "ever seeing Lester without a book or some research materials he was devouring. He did not need a formal education; he was doing that for himself."

Horton's approach to research was uniquely his own. He read a great deal but seldom very deeply. He might get as much from a copy of a popular magazine as from a history book, but when a fact or idea excited him, which was often, he seemed to remember it in context for years afterward. He became knowledgeable in a wide range of subjects and could speak intelligently, if not profoundly, about all of them. Learning for him was a delight, and he shared that delight with all who worked with him. There is a sense of research about his work through the years which was often commented upon by reviewers and which is a distinguishing mark of much of his artistic output.

For a while Lester teamed up with Madolyn King and Dorothy Wagner, two dancers he had met through Michio Ito. They appeared together in concert as the Dance Repertory Group. The program offered was mostly ethnic in nature, with a few idyllic pieces in a somewhat lyrical "moderne" style. The partnership was short-lived. The trio was handsomely costumed and attractive, but in 1931 the country's mood was not receptive to this kind of offering. A few years later, Horton and Wagner joined forces again and presented the Horton-Wagner Group for a few performances.

Jean Abel invited him to do another pageant the following year, this time on Aztec themes, and more important to his

career, she asked him to share in the teaching of a summer course
at the Little Theater of the Verdugos, located at the foot of the
Verdugo Mountains, northeast of Glendale. In the meanwhile,
she wondered if he would like to try his hand at directing a play.
She had convinced the Little Theater people to give him a chance
to direct, and the vehicle chosen was Conrad Seiler's *The Lady
in the Sack*. His efforts won for the group the first prize in a
one-act play tournament sponsored by the Los Angeles County
Drama Association. The judges were particularly impressed by
the novice director's innovative use of dance-like movement in
the production. It was, for Horton, an early attempt at creating
an integrated dance-drama form. The results must have been
good, for the formidable competition included groups that
worked in and around the motion picture industry.

The 1932 summer brochure for the Little Theater of the
Verdugos announced that Mr. Horton would teach "Primitive Dance
(Original), Complete Make-up and Ballet."

The first technique classes were so rugged in their demands
on flexibility, endurance, and strength that some of the students
literally feared that they would not survive the two-hour work
sessions. Lester was as likely to put jumps at the beginning as at
the end of class, but amazingly, no one seems to have died.
Later he got some books, studied a bit of anatomy, and became
a bit more reasonable in his demands. For a few days he would
talk about the importance of proper warm-up and breathing and
emphasize that movement from one position to another was
important, not only the positions themselves, as in ballet. Then
he would get excited about a new idea, forget warm-ups as he
understood them, and everyone would barely be able to move
for days afterward.

These earliest Horton classes were rough training, but in
record time the high school students were moving and moving
well. Jean Abel had furnished him with a group of strong,
pliant, and enthusiastic youngsters. With their hard work and

his imagination and freshly ignited ambitions he had them looking like dancers in only a few months.

The spark had come from the appearance of Mary Wigman in Los Angeles in 1932. This had a dizzying effect on Horton. If his first viewing of the Denishawn Dancers had nudged him into choosing dance as his life's work, the Wigman experience several years later gave him fresh inspiration and new direction. The great German dancer's sensitive and expressive use of percussion instruments opened a new world to Lester. In his own work he had used drums of various sizes and materials but always for the same purpose—as accompaniment to authentic and stylized American Indian dances. Now the aesthetic possibilities of percussion instruments as a motivation for and accompaniment to new dance ideas was revealed to him. He was especially intrigued by the brass gongs and after seeing Wigman, spent his last pennies to buy one in Los Angeles' Chinatown district. Wigman's treatment of space and the underlying mysticism of much of her work left him brimming with ideas and even more unanswered questions. He was to explore these ideas in the classroom and on the stage for several years to come.

With his characteristic anxiousness to try something new right after he learned about it, he created a few pieces which were little more than the trifle Karoun Tootikian humorously described in 1967, recalling a recital nearly forty years earlier:

> Lester gave each one of us a drum and had us walk a
> few steps, beat the drum, breathe deeply and kneel.
> Our expression, of course, had to be serious and intense.
> It was a little more than this but not much. We all
> bought drums and gongs after Wigman's visit.

At the close of the summer, an appearance at the Olympic Festival of the Dance at the Los Angeles Philharmonic Auditorium was announced by a new group, The Lester Horton Dancers. In addition to Horton, the dancers were: Doje Arbenz,

Brahm van den Berg, Jeanne Blodgett, Joewilla Blodgett, Arvin Bowne, William Bowne, Patricia Green, Maxine Heasley, Loys Safier, Elizabeth Talbot-Martin, Portia Woodbury, Karoun Tootikian, and Lavallete Tootikian. Several of these names were to appear on Horton programs for many years to come and, for at least a few, the association with him would change the course of their lives. In later years Horton dated his real artistic beginnings in California to the Little Theater of the Verdugos and to this group he had trained in the back-breaking summer course.

For the performance at the Philharmonic, which was then the principal house for touring companies in Los Angeles, Horton presented the American Indian *Kootenai War Dance* and *Voodoo Ceremonial*, inspired by W.B. Seabrook's book on Haiti, *The Magic Island*.* This fascinating book was for Horton more than merely the inspiration for a dance. The frank eroticism, the ritual sexual acts and blood sacrifices, the extraordinary earthy beauty of young women dancing barelegged with full, swinging skirts of crisp white ruffles glistening in the Haitian night, left indelible impressions on his mind which were to haunt him and recur constantly in his work in the years to come. It was a vision which became part of Horton's legacy to Alvin Ailey, who would transmute it to his own needs one day in his masterwork, *Revelations*. For "authentic" voodoo chants, Horton improvised with excerpts from *The Magic Island* mixed with a few Italian expletives which would not have gone too well with the censor, had there been one listening.

As a direct result of their successful appearance at the festival, the group was booked into the Paramount Theater in Los Angeles for a one-week engagement. They shared the billing with the comic Fuzzy Knight and a movie. Between shows the dancers spent their time designing, cutting, sewing,

*W.B. Seabrook, *The Magic Island* (New York: Harcourt Brace, 1929).

painting, trimming costumes, and building props for another
American Indian production, *Takwish, The Star Maker*. This
was a group effort which was to be the prototype of all
Horton's undertakings for the next twenty years. He honestly
needed the skills the dancers had and was willing and able to
teach them others which they needed to do the work. The
group simply could not afford a dancer whose only business
was to dance; everyone participated in all phases of the creative
process.

Horton wrote the scenario for *Takwish*, basing his plot
on California Indian folklore. He and Jean Abel collaborated
on the direction and costuming of the production, which was
described in the program as a dance drama. His costume
sketches reveal a splendid eye for color and design, but the
somewhat awkward detailing suggests that his exuberance surpassed his technical skill as an artist. The cast included twenty-
four dancers in addition to actors and singers. The outdoor
setting of the sycamore grove behind the Little Theater of the
Verdugos was ideal for the presentation, which was done at
night under the starlit California sky. From all verbal accounts
and reviews in the local press the presentation was a handsome
and successful one. Twenty percent of the box office receipts
was donated to the Glendale Unemployment Fund, a reminder
that the beginning of Lester Horton's group was concurrent with
the height of the Depression.

When Horton began teaching Saturday morning classes
at Norma Gould's studio on Larchmont Boulevard in Los
Angeles, the group from the Little Theater of the Verdugos
made the long trek from the Glendale area each week in order
to continue their work. The large studio was ideal, and most
of 1933 was spent there preparing new and varied concert
works. A small stage was used for workshop performances
in which Horton experimented with bold and colorful costumes

and lighting. Miss Gould, who had been Ted Shawn's first
dancing partner, coined the name "Dance Theater," which
Horton was to use a decade later. The orderly and immaculate
lady was, at first, dismayed by the thunderous sounds of the
percussion accompaniment for the Horton classes, and by the
barefooted students dragging their exhausted, sweaty bodies
through the halls where the genteel little girls she taught would
meet them head on. Horton, who knew how to charm the
ladies when necessary, somehow kept the peace. The young
Bohemian and the Victorian lady got along quite well together,
all things considered, and co-operated in the presentation of
local and touring artists in studio performances. Horton learned
a great deal about studio decorum and management from Miss
Gould, who was responsible and businesslike.

At this busy studio Horton came in further contact with
German developments in modern dance through guest teachers
Tina Flade (who had worked with Hanya Holm), Harald
Kreutzberg, and Yvonne Georgi. At this point Horton began
avidly reading anything he could find in print about the modern
dance in New York City. His knowledge of the work of Doris
Humphrey and Martha Graham came through articles in *American
Dancer, Dance Magazine,* and *Dance Observer.* At first he chose
to stay away when a Graham or Humphrey dancer taught guest
classes in Los Angeles, fearful that he would absorb too much
of their styles and lose the flow of originality that made his
own work uniquely his.

In a short while, that isolation would prove to be impossible. Those fine artists soon appeared on the West Coast
with their small groups and the inevitable happened. Horton
assimilated ideas from them just as he had from every other
movement source he had encountered. His power of absorption
was tremendous and his gift for elaboration, extensive. Soon
the new ideas were transmuted into his own broad, direct style—
"Hortonized," as it were.

Horton's classes at this time were built on progressions. After a warm-up which was often too brief, he would show a phrase and the dancers would vary the movement, traveling across the room according to his instructions. In this way a whole class might be built upon the exploration of one movement idea. The young teacher seemed to have an inexhaustible imagination, and two classes were seldom if ever alike; improvisation was second nature to him. Horton's inventiveness at this time was at once a great strength and weakness. Although the classes were most often exciting and exhilarating, they could also be chaotic and frenzied. The movement might be based on some ethnic materials, a balletic idea, or an on-the-spot inspiration. "Cross the floor as if you were a frog," he might call out. "No, bigger— louder— higher!" "He was using improvisation as a teaching tool as far back as 1932," a student during those years recalled. "He told us that the body would understand what the mind wanted it to do, and would be responsive if you didn't think too much." Occasionally a student would leave in disgust. Those who stayed on would leap higher and stay up longer than they themselves had imagined possible.

The vocabulary was based primarily on upper body movements, as Michio Ito's had been. A rolling action through the spine leading to undulations of the whole torso and pelvis would occur very often. Arms might be held parallel to each other or flexed at the elbow or wrist in a great variety of ways. A favorite position was one with arms held out to the side, shoulder level with elbows flexed at a ninety-degree angle. There was a pseudo-oriental forward slouch of the hip and a side inclination of the torso, reminiscent of East Indian sculpture from which it was doubtless borrowed. The focus was often on the hands and arms. Second and fourth positions of the feet were emphasized but complex leg gestures were not employed as the dancers moved through space. It was important *not* to look balletic.

In synthesizing what he had learned about the movement
of the primitives with the results of his current explorations,
something unique was emerging. The class work had a dynamic
and a daring that could not, at that point, have come out of
a carefully organized and thought-out conceptualization. It was
the result of a deeply intuitive nature at work. Conceptual
organization and clarification of his ideas would come later.

In addition to their classes, the Horton dancers had
weekly meetings to discuss their ideas in an effort to clarify
their objectives. Here Horton gave assignments to be worked
out individually and invited ideas encouraging the young dancers
to think creatively. The group would have long discussions
about the philosophy of the new dance. Why were they
dancing? Was it for themselves or for their audience? Where
did they fit into the evolving modern dance picture? Did they
want to grow along the lines of Mary Wigman, Martha Graham,
the Humphrey-Weidman group? Or were they something unique?
Bella Lewitzky has said:

> We felt that the body itself was the determining factor,
> and that it should be developed in as many ways as
> would be needed by any choreographer. Of course,
> this was a Utopian ideal, but we were very Utopian.
>
> So we set about to broaden the technique, rather than
> limit or even define it. We worked in the opposite
> register. We would get out on the floor and say, 'How
> many ways are there to go from up to down, how many
> paths are there?' And we would explore the ways of
> going from up to down. . . . We would do the same thing
> with moving across the floor. How many ways are
> there? What elements are involved in depth, in space,
> in time? Our entire vocabulary in those days was
> fashioned out of exploration on the part of the company.
> Then Lester would draw from what we had done, guiding

us toward the things he felt were significant and welding
them into technical studies.

> Then there were Lester's explorations in defying gravity.
> Tipping off balance, and holding the off-balance position
> if we possibly could. Falling and holding just a hair-
> breath [sic] off the floor. These were the kinds of
> things he would explore. He was extending the range
> of movement, forcing a resistance to gravity's pull. We
> would reach a point where we knew we could not
> achieve it, and then we did it. This was his demand.

The young dancers under Horton's direction were
evolving something related to, yet in its theatricality different
from, modern dance developments elsewhere. What they were
doing was equally exciting and valid. When it came to theater,
Horton's instinct bordered on the extraordinary. In Bill Bowne's
words, "In the mid-1930s we thought we had the message. We
were rich, prolific and colorful."

As was the case with most modern dance companies at
this time, the personnel was in a constant state of change; but
from the earliest days William Bowne stayed on, serving variously
as dancer, percussionist, librettist, costume designer, art director,
and—perhaps most importantly—company "stabilizer." Bowne
and Horton had developed a close personal relationship which
struck a good balance. Horton had been spoiled as a child. He
was, at times, willful and unreasonable. He often lacked discipline, even in relation to his own preferences. If there was a
little money, he spent it. If there was no food easily available,
he didn't eat. He either worked not at all or for two days
without sleep. This carelessness may have been one of the conditions of his creativity in those years, but it was an obstacle to
the kind of organization he needed for his work to be produced.

Bill Bowne, in contrast, came from a troubled home, and
had learned at an early age to accept responsibility and to

mediate problems. He was intelligent and good-natured, with
enough self-discipline for two. In his alliance with Horton, he
needed it. He had, from the beginning, been fascinated by
Horton's creativity and by his unconventional life style. After
a few years together, some of the best of each had been absorbed
by the other.

In *Dance to the Piper,** Agnes de Mille wrote that a young
artist needs a wall against which to grow. Although several
years younger than Horton and pursuing a college career in art,
Bowne found time to encourage, cajole, and advise his friend,
working tirelessly in whatever capacity he was needed. He
helped Horton to articulate his theories as they evolved and
constantly prodded him to bring greater order to his teaching
and choreography. Bowne was to be one of the founders of
Dance Theater in 1946.

A flash flood in 1934 washed away Horton's chicken
house. Katherine Stubergh rushed to the cottage to find him
standing forlorn, knee deep in mud, liberally sprinkled with
feathers, shells, and the plant and animal specimens he so dearly
loved to collect. Valuable costumes and props were lost, too.
It seemed practical now to move to the city.

The new home was a ramshackle two-story wreck
perched on a hill on First Street, near downtown Los Angeles.
The exposed plumbing was faulty, the roof leaked, and the
whole building tipped precariously to one side. It had, as a
matter of fact, been condemned but was rented to Horton for
$12 monthly. This abode was to be the hub of production
activities for Horton and his dancers during the next few years.
Soon the place was filled with the familiar Indian props,
blankets, drums, and other percussion instruments. Horton was
once again collecting, and now his acquisitions included inexpensive bits of folk art from nearby Chinatown, Little Tokyo,
and the Mexican Olvera Street. Often these bits of painted

*Agnes de Mille, *Dance to the Piper* (Boston: Little, Brown, and Company, 1951).

wood and clay would become the basis of an idea for a dance or a group of dances.

The house was shared by Bill Bowne, whose bottles of raw colors and art books helped give the place an attractive workshop atmosphere. And workshop it was. The bathtub was rainbow-hued from use as a dye vat. The downstairs space was used as a cutting and sewing room and for the construction of props, and the clothesline in the front yard often had dozens of weirdly-cut and dyed costumes drying in the warm sun. The usual pieces of social furniture were nowhere to be seen. At one time or another practically all of the dancers and some of their friends lived there.

In February, 1934, Horton was invited to direct Oscar Wilde's *Salome* at the Little Theater of the Verdugos. Once again his production placed first in the L.A. County Drama Association competition, this time against seventy competitors. One reviewer said that the entire production "articulated with the accent and rhythmic flow of the sensuous dance." Another described it as a verbal ballet. The excellent modular sets were designed by William Kline, who also played the part of John the Baptist. A graduate of the famous George Pierce Baker work-shop, he had worked in the professional theater in New York, and, believing Horton to be an unusually gifted man, he con-tinued to work with the company for two years. His bold lighting ideas were an intrinsic part of Horton's early theater-dance extravaganzas.

salome dances

The dance activities following the *Salome* success started out sanely enough with a performance for the Women's Club of Hollywood. Horton did a suite of new Oriental pieces, some lyric, some comic, a potpourri of short ethnic dances based on authentic materials and a few modern pieces, including an idyllic duet for himself and Elizabeth Talbot-Martin, *May Night*. He also restaged his 1932 success, *Voodoo*. Several similar engagements, plus evenings at Dance Theater, gave the company an opportunity to build a repertory and the assurance and confidence that can only develop in an ensemble which has numerous opportunities to perform together.

Talbot-Martin, a leading dancer in the group for several years, describes working with Horton at that time:

> It was as if we had been touched by some kind of
> magic. Creativity literally crawled out of us when we
> worked with Lester. Our Saturday sessions sometimes
> went for ten hours. If he called a five- or ten-minute
> break every few hours, we considered ourselves lucky.
> When performances were approaching we would use the
> breaks to cut and fit costumes. I don't know when or
> if we ate. We danced until we dropped, and when we
> went home, it was with a great sense of exhilaration

45

and accomplishment. Needless to say, our parents
took a dim view of this.

Some of the dancers were in college; a few were still in high
school.

When theatrical promoter Ed Perkins approached Horton
with the idea of forming the California Ballet Company, Horton
felt he had to accept in order for his work to progress beyond
the recital stage. He was ready for the next step. It meant
committing himself and his young group to a series of performances at the immense Shrine Auditorium in Los Angeles, one
of the largest theaters in the United States. Two of the showings
were scheduled just two weeks apart, and the whole thing was
only a few months off.
    With not even a remote possibility of public or private
support of any kind, this would be Horton's only conceivable
means in the foreseeable future of presenting his work in a
professional theater setting. It was a large step, but there seemed
to be no in-between steps possible. For a man who loved the
trappings of the theater, the prospect of working at last with
professional stagehands, lighting crew, and a live orchestra was
irresistible. It also meant publicity, which would focus the
attention of Los Angeles' theater-going public and the major
theater and music critics (there were none for dance) on his
work. He knew it was a win or lose venture, and feeling that
he had no choice, he plunged himself and his group into a frenzy
of preparation for the mammoth undertaking.
    A spectatular all-dance version of *Salome* was to be
featured in the first program. To attract attention to the production Perkins conceived the idea of a city-wide talent search
for beautiful girls to dance in the bacchanal which would precede
the "Dance of the Seven Veils." Perkins was a colorful "oper-
ator" of the old Hollywood school and wrote publicity releases

as often based on showmanship as on fact. Horton was touted
as a master choreographer from San Francisco whose staging of
ballets in Chicago and New York had brought him national
acclaim. At first Horton winced at the approach Perkins was
taking, but once he got into the spirit of things he threw in a
few imaginative stunts of his own. For instance, he had himself
"met" on his arrival at Union Station by the entire cast of the
production. The imaginative promoter had a field day changing
names: Joy Montandon, who was to play Salome, became "Joy
Montaya of the Vieux Carré, New Orleans, , formerly ballerina
with the exotic 'Samarkand Ballet'." Publicity promised
"beautiful girls who have danced in film musicals" and implied
that the "Dance of the Seven Veils" would be a bit salacious,
if not worse. Some legion for the protection of public morality
had duly alerted the police, who must have been disappointed
when Miss Montandon/Montaya danced with only one very long
veil, and was otherwise quite decently if flamboyantly attired.

The format of most programs in the series involved a
selection of short pieces followed by one long work. In the
first performance *Salome* was preceded by a reworking of the
Oriental pieces and some of Horton's more modern explorations.
It was a retrospective of the best of his works to date, minus the
American Indian material which was to come two weeks later.
For the occasion some of the dances were revised, some recast,
and a few retitled. Horton, never satisfied, was always making
improvements.

The costumes, designed by the choreographer, were outstanding, according to reviews. Colors and designs were bold,
imaginative, and sometimes startling. Handsome and unusual
effects were achieved by William Kline's lighting. In many of
the dances the performers accompanied themselves with percussion instruments and the sound of their own voices. Hand
claps and body slaps were also utilized. For some of the
pieces a lively old Victorian lady, Bertha Miller English, who

accompanied classes at the studio, bravely pounded a piano to the point of exhaustion in order to be heard in the gargantuan theater. Bits of Denishawn, Ito, and Wigman were to be seen in the choreography, but in Horton's broad, open, larger-than-life style, the material had an attractive vigorousness which brought repeated cheers from the suprisingly large audience.

Salome finished the program. In his first choreodrama, Horton created a gesture language which, though Oriental in character, was carefully tailored to the needs of the story. The movement of the individual characters was motivated by a consideration of their personalities as delineated in the Oscar Wilde play, and how these personalities would express themselves physically. The whole was realized in heroic strokes. Subtlety could not be a consideration. The Shrine stage, nearly a city block wide, was built to be large enough to accommodate a full circus. Much of the work was heavily pantomimic but facial expressions were kept blank. The drama was to come from the body or not at all. *Salome* may well have been the first attempt by any modern dance choreographer to sustain a dramatic story line in this way. It certainly was the first of many evenings of Lester Horton's Total Theater.

Salome had been advertised as a modern ballet, and one of the less enlightened reviewers, noting the bare feet and the unfamiliar style of the movement, referred to Horton as the "bad boy of ballet." The choreography in this first of many versions to come was relatively calm and restrained. It was only Horton's second encounter with the Salome character, which he would explore from different viewpoints and in different styles for the rest of his life.

Costumes designed by Portia Woodbury under Horton's supervision were starkly dramatic. An audible gasp went through the Shrine as Salome entered. The flesh colored bodice of her costume had nipples and a navel boldly expressed. Herod's costume had the look of a biblical robe, but one shoulder and

sleeve was slashed away. Elizabeth Talbot-Martin's Herodias had
a bare-backed halter top with full, sculptured padding sewn in to
give the lithe dancer a more womanly look. (By Talbot-Martin's
own recounting, in their haste the costumers had built only one
pattern for the padding and with true showmanship she went on
in the first performance with two left breasts.) An Orientally
tinged score was especially composed for *Salome* by Constance
Boynton, and by Horton's request the music was played from
the wings so that the focus would be entirely on the dancers.
The effect was a startling one for the time and was mentioned in
numerous reviews.

The notices, though generally extremely enthusiastic and
encouraging, criticized some of the work for pretentiousness,
repetition, and affectation. Costumes and stage effects were
consistently lauded, while Horton, who danced Herod, Elizabeth
Talbot-Martin, Joy Montaya, Toni Masarachia, and Brahm van
den Berg were singled out for special praise. The most prophetic
of the critics suggested that the evening be regarded as "more
interesting as a promise and a beginning than as a complete
realization." As for the dozens of beautiful girls in the bacchanal,
the kindest reviewer, describing them as "young ladies of obviously recent dance achievement," suggested that there were too
many of them and that they had not helped the effectiveness
of the production. This was to be a problem in many of
Horton's presentations through the years. He dearly loved to
mass large numbers of people on the stage, and obstinately
refused to listen to advice on the subject.

Brahm van den Berg was the star of the evening. He
was lauded in the press for his sensitive and expressive interpretation and comprehensive technical accomplishment. The son
of a well-known Dutch concert pianist, van den Berg was a
natural dancer who was barely out of his teens at the time. He
was one of the first of many gifted dancers who were given an
opportunity by Horton to excel on stage when scarcely more

than beginners. Indeed most of the splendid roles Horton created were not for himself but for the youngsters in the group with the best potential. It was part of his talent to mold these inexperienced dancers into artists as he developed material that showed them to best advantage. In a situation unique in the early years of modern dance, a highly gifted and prolific choreographer had no wish to put himself in the place of the leading dancer.

Horton was not well built for dancing. He was tall and barrel-chested with a long, extremely flexible torso, short legs, and a tendency to overweight. Costumes were always cleverly designed to conceal his body line. Bella Lewitzky has said, "He did not dance well himself, but he danced beautifully." William Bowne recalls, "He was a most imperfect dancer, but a memorable performer, if uneven. An American Indian dance or one of his Oriental compositions would be performed magnificently on most occasions." Critics during the mid and late 1930s were generous in their praise of his effectiveness on stage. His portrayal of Herod in *Salome* was described in the *Los Angeles Times* as "imbued with dramatic strength, never deviating from a drunken, half-mad character sunk in sensuality." The roles that he wisely chose for himself were either dramatic or satiric in nature. Apparently his dramatic projection was outstanding. He retired from active performance in the late 1930s.

The program two weeks later fared less well but was saved by a reprise of the voodoo piece which had been created for the Olympics dance event. The dancers, wearing black shrouds and green masks, were accompanied by huge drums played by other dancers on stage. They entered with a slow procession down a long ramp. Horton was intrigued by the effect of the interplay of levels and was to use it often. Abstractions of black trees were painted on a backdrop.

When Horton revised a piece, the revision was often a complete one. Some of the previous rendition might survive,

but in a scarcely recognizable form. As his choreographic range
broadened he could see no reason for resurrecting movement
materials which he could improve upon, and this new version of
Voodoo Ceremonial was much more sophisticated than the first one
had been.

Florence Lawrence, writing in the *Los Angeles Examiner,*
said, "His grasp of elemental emotions as portrayed in the
dance, his use of symbols, of mysticism and hypnotic suggestion
all serve to make this quartet of semi-barbaric dances excep-
tional." His *Aztec Ballet* looked like German modern dancing
to one writer. Another said, "It had moments of daring
originality and downright genius . . . but was it Aztec?" "Too
many different ideas danced to the same steps," suggested a
third. Another physically handsome pageant-like production, the
Painted Desert Ballet, featured in the cast Thelma Babitz, who
later joined the Martha Graham Company, and Toni Masarachia,
virtually untrained but an excellent primitive dancer. The work,
with a score by Homer Grunn, who had done the *Xochitl* score
for Ted Shawn, suffered a critical fate similar to that of the
Aztec Ballet.

Viola Hegyi (Swisher), who was to become an enthusiastic fan of Horton's work, summed up the critical consensus by
writing: "The modern dance is in its early, formative stages,
remaining nebulous in expression, if not in intent . . . The
technique of this new dance is not yet rich enough to make it
an eloquent means of expression." ·Yet she went on to praise
Horton's effort and encouraged the group to continue working.
Even the harshest critics seemed to sense that something important was happening. They respected what they understood to
be the motivation behind the sometimes pretentious gropings
of Horton's work and were more than willing to allow for the
possibility that a great new talent was in the process of
evolving. Indeed, they said so.

Horton learned two things from this Shrine Auditorium
experience. He learned not to try two completely different

major concerts in one month and that ideas which work well in outdoor settings for relatively unsophisticated audiences do not necessarily translate well to the concert stage. In his frantic rush to complete the balance of the commitments at the Shrine in the fall, he had gone beyond his own development as a choreographer and likewise beyond the technical skills of many of his dancers.

In the last program of the series, Horton gave Brahm van den Berg an opportunity to choreograph. The piece was *An American in Paris*, with Gershwin's music and handsome black and white costumes by Elizabeth Talbot-Martin. One clever reviewer wrote, "If this is truly indicative of an American in Paris, that largely explains the bad impression foreigners have of Americans abroad." Few of the critics seem to have disagreed. It was the last time Horton ever presented anyone else's choreography on one of his own programs. The same witty reviewer, obviously not a fan, referred to Horton's largely revised (and much sexier) *Salome* as "Sallow Mae." Horton was amused, but from then on she was known in successive revisions only by the English pronunciation.

Audiences were considerably more impressed than critics. They liked what they were seeing and came in ever-increasing numbers. Thanks in part to Ed Perkins' publicity and to the attention the performances had received from the press, Horton's class enrollment swelled. His name was becoming synonomous with modern dance in Los Angeles. The group was officially organized as a cooperative at this time, and the name Horton Dance Group was adopted.

After each concert, when bills were paid and Perkins had taken his rather large share, Horton was shocked to find himself nearly where he had started financially. He was learning that dance concert work, even with large audiences, did not make money. One was lucky to break even and come out with musical scores and costumes paid for.

After the hectic series at the Shrine several dancers from the Little Theater of the Verdugos group left to concentrate on other work. New names on the program included Renaldo Alarcon, Bruce Burroughs, Maury Armstrong, Eleanor Brooks, Kita Van Cleve, Jeri Faubion, Ana Kurgans, Mary Meyer, Ethel Nichols, and Bella Lewitzky. Alarcon, a Mexican-American, became the leading male dancer. He replaced Brahm van den Berg, who came and went a great deal with lucrative film work now available to him. Kuuks Walks Alone had stayed on from one of the early pageants, and several other American Indians danced with the group at one time or another. Unselfconsciously and without fanfare, Horton had created the first interracial dance company in the United States. At no time did he ever type-cast a dancer based on color. He loved variety in human beings as in all things and looked at dancers for talent, dedication, and the capacity for hard work. Renaldo Alarcon had been chosen for the same reason that Carmen de Lavallade and James Truitte were later given leading roles; all had outstanding promise which Horton felt he could help to fulfill.

Throughout his adult life Horton could not bear to hear jokes about minority groups, and if someone started to tell one he would leave the room. In most of his dealings Horton was a gentle and lovable man. To be rebuked by him in this way was far more effective than a tongue lashing would have been. Had he lived to see his work discussed under "The Black Dance" in Walter Terry's *The Dance in America,** he would doubtless have been both amused and proud; amused because he was not black and proud to be in the fine company of Bill "Bojangles" Robinson and ethnologist, dancer, choreographer Pearl Primus.

Riding high on the Shrine successes, the Group had six major engagements in Los Angeles in the next year and at least that many showings for women's clubs in close-by cities such as Long Beach and Redlands. An overview of the choreographic offerings on these programs suggests that Horton was spreading

*Walter Terry, *The Dance in America* (New York: Harper & Row, 1956).

his talents very thin over a broad spectrum of movement styles.
Along with American Indian pageants, there were lyric, Oriental,
and Mexican thematic materials, the latter in his own emerging
modern style. At this point in his career, the need to create
significant artistic dance works was secondary to his need to
explore effects that could be created with the elements of
theater. By not limiting himself to the creation of serious works,
he was able to grow at his own pace and slowly develop his own
style. Meanwhile, he was pleasing a large and enthusiastic
audience. As a theater person, he recognized his responsibility
to entertain, and by and large he was successful.

The movement vocabulary, however, was not keeping up
with his choreographic output. His dancers could move well in
a variety of styles, but his own work was growing in variety and
outward appearance rather than in depth. In later years this
versatility would qualify him well for work in films and night-
clubs as well as on the concert stage, but now it led a few of the
more astute critics to voice some complaints along with their
praise and encouragement. "Once you've seen him, you've seen
him all," wrote one. From another, "There is a need for greater
variation in technique. It is impossible to expect pelvic convul-
sions to express all emotions." The critics in Los Angeles
continued to watch over him with a combination of pride and
interest but they seldom indulged him with unqualified praise.

For one of the performances Horton tried his hand at
choreographing Ravel's "Bolero," to which he gave a gypsy
setting. According to Bella Lewitzky, if you could walk and
were taking classes with Horton you were cast in *Bolero*. It was
more a of motion, sound, and color theater event than a conventional choreographic work. The piece opened with a solo figure
on stage performing a very simple step in lightly saturated cool-
colored lighting. As other dancers fed in, the colors intensified
and changed, building dramatically. At the climax, there were
dozens of performers in attractive formation gyrating on the

stage in rich, deeply saturated areas of light. The *Herald* critic
wrote, "This daring, unconventional interpretation . . . bewildered
with its peculiar rhythms, almost blinded with clanking colors
and smote the ear with cacaphonic woe. But it was different
and had the energy of genius, no matter how far gone wrong.
What it lacked was a general design to bind it."

In the last months of 1934, Horton started work on the
revision of the *Aztec Ballet* into the expanded and thematically
changed *Mound Builders*. It is with this piece that a new and
important trend can be seen in his work, the shift to more contemporary concerns in both subject matter and choreographic
treatment. Pageantry is no longer an end in itself but a format
for the exploration of the social and cultural heritage of a
people, and there is a pronounced emergence of a radical political
consciousness. *Mound Builders*, with a Mexican setting, was
divided into two sections. Section one, "The Plumed Serpent,"
was a series of Aztec-inspired celebrations of the Sun, the Earth,
and the Maguey plant, finishing with a Dirge. "Post Conquest,"
the second section, builds from "Black Madonna," a primitive
reaction to Christianity, to "Dances for the Revolution," "Dance
for Zapata," and "Dance into Solidarity."

The last two dances are described thus by a local critic:
" 'Dance to Zapata,' ostensibly a tribute to the popular hero, is
at once the striking of a note of revolution and a prelude to the
'Dance into Solidarity,' which is a clear and forcible statement
of Mexican defiance . . . oppressed groups come together into a
single body and demand the rights of the people in a stirring
climax of union."

In 1935 new additions to the repertory included *Dictator*,
an anti-fascist group piece, and *The Mine*, inspired by a newspaper article about a mine disaster. *The Mine* was divided into
"Dependents," "Women Waiting," and "Strike." The "Women
Waiting" section, one of Horton's finest early pieces, was
described in *The American Dancer*: "A group of women waiting

at a mine shaft after a disaster; with a modicum of motion and
no facial expression the terrific emotional strain was clearly
transferred to the audience."

The third important new dance created for the 1935
season was *Art Patrons*, described in programs as "satire on the
snobbery in the theater, a gibe at outworn criteria, critical
pedantry, the vicious censor, the pompous art lecturer and all
the impedimenta of a lingering decadence."

Within a year of the success of his delightfully decadent
Salome production Horton had joined the "revolution" and was
attacking decadence.

dancers unite!

The relatively tiny colony of serious modern dancers in Los Angeles was a counterpart in miniature of the competitive and partisan New York dance world, in which insults were magnified and misunderstandings between groups frequent. However, in times of national emergency petty grievances are often put aside to face the larger enemy. During the years of the Great Depression several modern dance groups in New York and Los Angeles allied themselves with the New Dance League described in brochures as "a national organization dedicated to a fight against war, fascism and censorship and devoted to raising the dance to its highest artistic and social levels."

The stated objectives may sound like strange bedfellows, but in the dismal and depressing 1930s modern dance was many things to many people, and to most it was a harbinger of a new era. The fiercely independent attitude of the pioneers of the new dance attracted such enthusiastic young devotees as the two quoted in a *New York Post* interview in 1936. Asked why they were studying dance at the New Dance League, a male art student said he felt, "We must express everyday problems for the betterment of mankind," and a young model replied, "I want to express life today in all its squalor and despair. I want to express the ideas and beliefs of the workers."

Members of the Young Communist League and similar organizations were flocking to modern dance studios on both coasts. They would get into heated discussions of exploitation of the working class, the beating up of union organizers, and most frightening of all, the growth of Fascism in Nazi Germany and its spread to America. The only help for society, they believed, lay in broad, sweeping social and political change. The Communist Party was for many young people a symbol of hope, of a possibility for something more than mere survival.

During these difficult years many dancers, writers, and graphic artists used their work as an outlet to express specific political ideologies. Not only did the works tell what was wrong, but often they suggested some fairly specific mode of action as a remedy, i.e., unite, rebel, strike. These "agitprop" (agitation-propaganda) art works were created and presented with an unprecedented missionary zeal and sometimes with a good deal of eloquence. However, one observant dance reviewer in Los Angeles who attended a concert which seemed to have innumerable dances directed against tyranny and oppression, tells us that no one seemed to leave with his basic attitudes changed. Those who responded favorably to the not-so-subtle symbolism cheered wildly for the dancers. The uninitiated shrugged the whole thing off as danced lectures or rabble rousing.

In New York City the audiences were much more in tune with protest dance, and at least some of the critics seemed to be more than understanding of what was going on, as was evidenced by the tone of these excerpts from a review of Anna Sokolow's works in the April, 1937 *Dance Observer:*

> The first of the new dances was a solo, *Case History No.* — (Riegger), which turned a searchlight on the progression from poverty and unemployment to the career of petty crime which is all too often the lot

of the underprivileged. The opening movements of this
dance suggested very well the energy and loneliness of
youth trying to adjust itself to false and unfriendly
conditions; the sense of futility and the growing despair
in the youth become the force which drives him toward
defiant and anti-social acts.

And for another work, *Excerpts From a War Poem*:

In clear choreographic style and pattern, with her flair
for putting bitter comment in gently humorous guise,
and with a concept and viewpoint equal to the scope
of her subject matter, she has composed one of the most
stirring indictments against war that has been seen in
dance. No "battle scenes" here; no tear-jerking melo-
drama, no preaching. She has taken the essence of
fascism, embodied in a poem extolling the beauties of
war, and has plucked this expression of an ideology
mercilessly apart, line by line, exposing a ruthlessness,
a savagery, and a masochistic blindness underlying this
viewpoint which are appalling in their implications.

Was Bolshevism rampant in modern dance at the time?
Martha Graham expressed her own attitude, if not that of all
of the members of her group, on the question of whether or
not all modern dance was, indeed, red, rabid, and radical.

Dancing reflects social conditions but that doesn't mean
it is a vehicle for any kind of propaganda. The instrument
is your body, and your body lives in this time. It is
influenced by the life, the conditions of the moment.
Life is now changing fast. A new set of symbols is being
created. People have a new attitude toward life, and this
new attitude, this new awareness is reflected in the
modern dance.

Horton, on the other hand, was among those who believed that dance could not reflect social conditions and at the same time avoid being propaganda. In his own work for the next several years he felt a strong motivation to create dances based not on abstract form or elusive emotion but on what he referred to as "vital experiences." He later wrote with atypical grimness, "The substantial realities about which he [the choreographer] can conduct a serious investigation shall be the legitimate material of his dance." For him these substantial realities were social and political. The intense commitment of Party workers in his group and the strength of his belief that the central humanistic ideas were morally correct led to a radical change in his work over a period of just a few months. He gave up work on his beloved pageant-like compositions and ethnically-based dances to concentrate more intently on developing a style based on a new purpose: to make dances which would influence and, perhaps, instruct.

Even at its most extreme, Horton's alliance with the "left" was more of the heart than of the mind. He was too much of a romanticist to be a typical 1930s "intellectual," and was actually quite bored by abstract political discussion. He never joined the Party, partially out of an avowed abhorrence of blind chauvinism and partly because the heavy Marxist theoretical ideologies simply did not interest him.

The year of Horton's most significant artistic change was 1935. He had done the last American Indian story-telling pageant in his career, *Rain Quest*. Dances which had served him well for many years, such as the "Hoop Dance," "Prairie Chicken Dance," and "Corn Dance," were retired from his repertory after their use in the "Ceremonial" section of this work. A group of lyrical dances featuring such titles as *May Night* composed by Palmgren, *Dance of Parting* by Davico, and Satie's *Second Gnossienne*, often shown that year, give us an idea that a yearning toward lyricism marked Horton's transition

from pageants to protest dances. The romantic *May Night*, a
duet for Horton and Talbot-Martin, was often singled out for
high praise.

By 1936 Horton had emerged as a choreographer
intensely involved in the problems of his time. "The dances
are propaganda," wrote the *American Dancer* critic, "but they
are good dances in themselves." *Dictator* was the quintessential
agitprop piece in the repertory during this era. From contemporary accounts it appears to have been a powerful and
direct piece with little left to the imagination. The far right
press in Los Angeles, which seemed to have no quarrel with
Nazi Party branches in the city, took special pains to attack the
Horton Dance Group regularly and used publicity pictures from
this anti-fascist work as evidence of the company's dangerous
"red" activities. In one article, the word *cooperative* is used
contemptuously as proof of the group's subversiveness.
Political activists in the dance world of the 1930s were to be
sought out by the House Un-American Activities Committee
in the early 1950s. When questioned by that infamous group,
Bella Lewitzky rose to her full 5' 2½" and said, "Gentlemen,
I am a dancer, not a singer." That is all she said.

Frank Eng tells us that when Horton was told a few
years later that they could have their names removed from the
"grey" list by a relatively simple procedure, his response was to
march out of the room and slam the door with an intensity that
shook the walls of the theater.

Flight From Reality, premiered in 1936, was interesting
as a reflection of Horton's growth as an artist. It was a group
of solos for himself which were in essence a manifesto of separation
from his past. In one of these, "Escape into the Exotic," he mocked
the pseudo-Orientalisms of the Denishawn era with what one
reviewer described as an almost bitter reproach. (Many years
later Horton would amuse his dancers with a remembered

fragment which he called "Miss Ruth [St. Denis] Hanging Out the Laundry," complete with arm ripples and Hindu mudras. In "The Ivory Tower" he expressed his contempt for those who close their eyes to the conflicts of the real world.

It was dance-with-a-message at its peak, and Horton went at it with a vengeance. This new phase of his work precipitated a rapid turn-over in the company. When Elizabeth Talbot-Martin got the message, she bowed out to develop a distinguished career as a dancer, mime, actress, and teacher. Within a year of her departure from the Horton group her picture was on the cover of *American Dancer*, the first, but not the last of Horton's progeny to appear there.* Joy Montandon accepted a marriage proposal and retired from dance. With their departure Horton lost two of his finest dancers who were in a sense not replace-able, for each was completely individual in approach to move-ment, and roles had been built for and around them. Horton never again performed *May Night*, and when Bella Lewitzky became the new Salome little trace remained of the choreography designed for her predecessor. Lewitzky and another fine dancer in the company, Eleanor Brooks, were moved up to fill the front ranks.

In 1934 Bella Lewitzky had enrolled in Lester Horton's classes at the Norma Gould Studio. She had tried ballet as Horton himself once had, and for her also this was not the answer. At the ballet studio someone told her about an insane man who had his dancers moving all over the place. She was promised that it was not at all like ballet. Lewitzky, still in her teens, fell in love with what she saw in Lester Horton's class on the first visit. Indeed, the dancers *were* moving all over the place. William Bowne was playing loudly and angrily at the percussion rack. Suddenly he threw the beater halfway across the room, screamed something at the teacher and left.

American Dancer, August, 1936.

Although not an accomplished dancer himself, Bowne had strong ideas about teaching and if something was not going the way he thought it should, he let it be known. Horton heeded as often as not. Lewitzky later said:

> It was the noisiest class I've ever heard. They did progressions only. There was hardly any recognizable technique at that point, that I can remember. Lester would start a movement and it would go on and on. I said, 'This is for me!' It was wild and wonderful.

Lewitzky came to her first classes equipped with a fine body, tremendous enthusiasm, and a commitment to dance which would prove ideal for the association with Horton, which was to last for fifteen years. Within less than a year of her first appearance as a member of the ensemble, she was dancing leading roles to favorable critical notice. She became invaluable, too, in the creation of new works. Moving in front of his dancers, Horton would indicate where he felt a sequence of movement should go and perhaps demonstrate a portion of what he wanted. Two of the Horton dancers of this period were especially responsive to this method of working, Brahm van den Berg and Lewitzky. They would not only fulfill the sequence to his satisfaction but in time, through a combination of keen intuition and familiarity with his approach, they could embellish the movement so that it was a completed phrase. If it didn't work, they kept trying. It was a unique creative process which Horton dancers of that era remember with awe to this day. When Lewitzky was unable to satisfy Horton or herself, she went off to a corner to work, sometimes for hours, on a single phrase or portion of a phrase. Dancers in the group would say, "If Bella can't do a movement, nobody can." This determination and un-willingness to accept limitations led her to become a most extra-

ordinary virtuoso dancer. Thirty-five years later, Clive Barnes, reviewing her 1971 concert debut in New York, was startled into
admitting that not all of American dance took place in that city. He
called her one of America's great modern dancers and wrote of her
remarkable technique and most exquisite natural sense of movement. This superb talent was first recognized by Dorathi Bock
Pierre, who wrote in the May 1936 *American Dancer*, "Bella
Lewitzky . . . shows promise of becoming a really fine dancer
of the modern school." By 1937, there was scarcely a review
that did not single her out for praise, and by 1940 Pierre wrote
prophetically, "She has it in her power to create an immortal
place for herself among the great American dancers."

Eleanor Brooks was another especially gifted dancer in
the group. She moved with a warm and emotional legato
quality, in contrast to Lewitzky's volatile brilliance. A fine
performer, she had a kind of personal tranquillity which was
rare in the tempestuous dance world of the mid-1930s. Both
dancers were extremely idealistic, hardworking, and uncompromising, and were not afraid to challenge the inventive Horton,
who was often unreasonable and stubborn. Lewitzky recalled
years later:

> If he felt a criticism was justified he would heave a great
> sigh, look very crestfallen, and then get to work making
> the needed changes. We genuinely loved him and never
> challenged him in a way that would cause him to forget
> that love. We valued him highly and he trusted us.

The three worked together with a deep mutual affection
and respect. The young ladies cheerfully called themselves
"Horton's Kosher Nuns" and worked for him with just that
kind of devotion.

In 1936 the Lester Horton Dance Group moved into
their own second-floor studio at 7377 Beverly Boulevard. It was

large, light and airy and had a fine resilient floor. The walls
were painted terra cotta and cerulean blue. There were no
mirrors, on the theory that movement should be learned
kinesthetically rather than by staring at one's reflection. The
studio had a barre, but it was installed several inches higher
than the academic ballet barre. The rent of $50 monthly was
seldom paid in a lump sum. Partial payment was made at
the beginning of the month and the rest as tuition money
trickled in. Money generated by the school was often needed
to cover concert costs.

Among the classes offered were music for dance, speech,
orchestra, and dance composition, with special classes for men,
for actors, and for teachers. Classes for company members
included current events, the history of art, music and dance,
scene design, make-up, and partner support. When the company
classes did not concern dance or theater directly, Horton tended
to be passive in his participation. Although the group remained extremely committed politically as well as artistically, Bella Lewitzky
recalls that Horton often seemed distracted when politics were
under discussion at any length. William Bowne was in charge
of the company classes Horton did not teach. The format was
generally one which encouraged group involvement.

If Horton was launching a new work, he would tell his
group about his ideas. When a dance about a particular culture
was projected, the art, music, history, and movement patterns
of the people were studied. It was understood that company
members would do research assignments and share their findings
at the next meeting. This work was not intended to affect
Horton's choreography directly, but rather to give the dancers
a frame of reference upon which to build characterizations.
Underlying the philosophy of their cooperative effort was the
idea that though they didn't have much materially, they could
share what they did have and they could learn together.

When Bella Lewitzky started teaching, the techniques
began to take a more formal shape. Where Horton was inspired

but often vague in his directions, she prodded for order and clarification. She criticized his work for sometimes being care-less. He complained that her teaching was balletic in approach and could potentially cut off a student's spontaneity. In the sparks that flew between his wealth of creativity and her need for form, a splendid training technique began to evolve.

Horton read about and was deeply impressed by the work of the Dutch physical culturist, Dr. Bess Mensendieck, who regarded the body as architecture and was exploring the relationship between posture and good health. He turned his serious attention, at last, to a consideration of the structure of the human body and defined his new aims in an interview:

> I am sincerely trying now to create a dance technique based entirely on corrective exercises, created with a knowledge of human anatomy; a technique which will correct physical faults and prepare a dancer for any type of dancing he may wish to follow; a technique having all the basic movements which govern the actions of the body; combined with a knowledge of the origin of movement and a sense of artistic design.

These searchings apparently did not result in a decrease in his demands on the stamina of his dancers. A few years later, James Mitchell presented him with a skeleton labelled "Me after six weeks with Horton" and Joyce Trisler recalls many occasions in the early 1950s when she thought during a grueling rehearsal, "This man is going to kill me. I could die right here, and he wouldn't even care."

Horton's was a streamlined technique, designed to build competent dancers in the shortest possible time. There were exercises for every movable part of the face, the fingers, the toes; joint actions of the body were emphasized and a minimum of effort was spent on minutiae. The uncomplicated directness

of primitive movement as he had come to understand it was at
the base of many of the important exercises. The emphasis
was on performance. If the class was working on *pliés*, he
expected them to be performed. "It is too late," he said, "to
start when you get to the theater. There are other problems
to be solved there."

His desire to train dancers quickly was based more on
practical than on aesthetic considerations. Working as he did
in close proximity to the movie industry, he ran the risk of
losing his dancers to lucrative film work. Even with his con-
centrated teaching techniques it took him well over a year to
coax the growth of an aspiring dancer into the appearance of
an acceptable performer. He was extremely resentful of
youngsters who left him to take professional work soon after
they learned how to move well. Becoming a member of the
Horton Dance Group was like joining a family. Once accepted,
one was fed, worried over, cared for, and jealously guarded. If
a dancer later decided to leave the fold, it was a grim and
painful affair for all concerned. Horton so completely depended
upon the loyalty of company members that departure came to
be seen as desertion.

When Benjamin Zemach, who had come to the United
States with the Habima Theater, sent out a call for dancers for
a Hollywood Bowl production, Horton, in the midst of rehearsals
for an important performance, firmly announced that any of his
dancers who attended the audition would not be welcome back
at the studio. Acting from somewhat less justifiable motives, he
also called a rehearsal on the evening of Elizabeth Talbot-Martin's
first independent solo concert.

In spite of all the vexations of his position Horton
worked on an even emotional keel most of the time, but any
real or imagined breach of loyalty to him or the company
made him inwardly furious. He handled his anger or
annoyance indirectly by reassigning a job or, in extreme cases,

by recasting a role. He could overwork dancers at a rehearsal and use this as retaliation. The harshest thing he could do to anyone in the group was to withdraw his favor. This was crushing to most of his dancers, who loved and respected him. Almost inevitably Horton's anger was short-lived, and when it passed he would carry on as if nothing had happened. He was thirty years old and had assumed the responsibility of a school, a company, and the liberal education of a group of dancers who were, in some cases, only a few years younger than he was. Horton was not always just, nor were his dancers always considerate. A flareup of tempers would come with the fervor of a family quarrel, and the accumulation of past grievances added intensity to the anger. It was at these times that Bill Bowne would be called in as peacemaker. On more than one occasion he was able to help to resolve a troubled situation which seemed, at the time, irreversible. For the most part, the group was closely knit and dedicated. They adored their teacher who had won their respect because he had first won their love.

Horton and Bowne lived in a tiny room beneath the studio. By saving the monthly expense of keeping an apartment, he could afford to launch one more piece of choreography for the next concert, or replace some badly worn costumes, or perhaps add another piece or two to his ever-growing collection of percussion instruments. Remembering his own years of extreme privation, he gave numerous scholarships. He was generous to a fault in this way and had been since the Little Theater of the Verdugos days. Most of the modest income from the school went into studio expenses, theater rental, props and scenery, fabric for new costumes, and the innumerable other expenses of production. Breaking even financially from a major performance had become only a dim hope, and making a profit was scarcely thought of. During these lean years there were no stringent union regulations that, while protecting the dancers, would have made it impossible to create anything from which to protect them. There were no grants, no foundations to call upon. One emptied one's pockets and begged and borrowed the rest.

A week or two before performances, Katherine Stubergh knew she could expect a small delegation from the Horton Dance Group to come to her studio for paint, scraps of fabric, plaster of Paris, and whatever else they might need. She and her mother gave generously, knowing that the dancers had almost no money for such things. A few days later an urgent phone call would come through from Horton, asking for a loan for some unanticipated expense which threatened to cancel the performance if not paid, C.O.D. The Stuberghs would oblige. No sooner was the loan repaid than the ritual would be repeated. The support of such constant friends as the Stuberghs was the only financial aid Horton was ever to know. Bill Bowne has said, "It was our individual contributions that kept the thing going financially. It seems incredible to me now, but that was all we had to work with." And, from Bella Lewitzky:

> No one ever entered dance for money in those days, it was absolutely unheard of. We came to the Dance Theater because we were gaining something very definite there. There were places I could have gone to earn money, but they didn't interest me. So I didn't go, nor did the others. We worked with Lester because that was what we wanted to do. I think that was the attitude everywhere then. Otherwise there would have been no modern dance.

This period of idealism and dedication resulted in a brief but meaningful golden age in all the arts in the United States. It provided the spirit in which the Lester Horton Dance Group could thrive, creating an atmosphere in which Horton, through trial and error, could develop his work.

One fringe benefit of being a member of the Horton
Dance Group was being treated to one of Lester Horton's
memorable, often improvised, gourmet meals. He had through
the years become an extraordinary "shoe-string" cook, and
though he rarely set eyes on a cookbook his inventiveness in the
kitchen became legendary. With only a few dollars to spend he
could put together enough food for a company feast during one
of the marathon pre-performance rehearsals. It was understood
that anyone who had a bit of spare money would make a contribution. In the rare case of a windfall someone might even
show up at rehearsal with a treat of steak or chops. A gallon
of inexpensive wine usually finished the meal, and after a round
of well-deserved praise for the chef, the group would get back
to the studio and work until they fell from exhaustion. (For
recipe, see page 239.)

At the studio Horton had his hand in every aspect of
production. With William Bowne he designed sets and costumes.
The props were generally his exclusive province. Not content
with commercially prepared dyes, he bought the ingredients and
created his own. It was not uncommon to come upon him, in
the middle of the night, whistling through the spaces between
his teeth, his hands and arms tinted in the ferocious hues that
appealed to him. Company members were taught to do batik
and tie-dyeing thirty years before they became popular crafts.
It seldom occurred to anyone to ask him where he had learned
these crafts. It was just taken for granted that Lester knew how
to do such things.

Horton's easy rapport with members of minority ethnic
groups living in the Los Angeles area was a revelation to the
members of the company. Integration, for him, had never been
something to work toward; it simply was a fact of life. From
the time of his childhood it was quite natural for him to seek
out and befriend people with exotic ethnic backgrounds
living wherever he happened to live. His sincere curiosity and

open-mindedness made him welcome in shops, restaurants, and theaters hardly ever visited by outsiders. He was often invited to share the festival days of different ethnic groups, not as an observer but as a participant.

A jaunt with Horton to the Mexican, Japanese, or Chinese sections of Los Angeles meant finding exciting shops, excellent food, and sometimes unique theater. More importantly, it meant a broadening of taste and awareness and the development of the ability to meet and relate to people outside of one's own milieu. Bella Lewitzky recalled:

> My first introduction to Chinese food and customs was through him. When we went to Chinatown, the merchants brought out their best wares for him. The older ones, very mandarin, would bring out priceless things for Lester. In Japantown it was the same. The minute Lester walked in, out came the obis, out came the yardage. He knew the Japanese merchants and artists, he was familiar with their legends, with their people, with their folkways, with their musical instruments, with their modes of movement, with their holidays, with their crafts.
>
> He knew the Mexican-Americans in the same way. We went into Mexican-American homes, we knew their songs, we had a Mexican-American member in the company, Renaldo Alarcon, who taught us their dances.
>
> He knew the Negro community, and was welcome in their homes. We often went to places like Club Alabam where they would do a special show for us if we came after our own performance, because Lester was always welcome and his company was always welcome. He knew their material, from jazz on up, although he made his own versions of it and we never looked like jazz dancers. He knew their beat, their kind of music. People like Thurston Knudson and Augie Goupil taught us about their drums and the rhythm of the islands. He brought

people like this into the theater. This was the man I
knew in those years.

At Christmas time Lester would make his version of
Della Robbia wreaths, and friends would wait for these
to arrive. He used fresh fruit in them, so we would have
the fragrance of lemon and apple in the house all the
time. Then he added pine and bits of Mexican glass, so
there would be the green and the brilliant glass and the
fragrance of pine and fruit, which would last throughout
the entire season. This was typical of him. With a more
than busy schedule, he would find time to make these
beautiful gifts.

In the mid-1930s the traditional relationship between
music and dance was being questioned by modern dancers on
both coasts. Several independent artists had already performed
in complete silence in order to declare their emancipation from
European musical tradition. In the process of looking for a new
balance, choreographers often seemed willing and eager to sub-
ordinate music to their own whims with little respect for the
integrity of the musical composition.

Horton felt that neither extreme was desirable. In a
1936 interview he said:

> We . . . believe that a situation far more fertile in
> possibilities is the making of new music simultaneously
> with the making of choreography . . . in welding the two
> elements, movement and sound, it is possible to achieve
> a homogeneity which is a stronger entity than either
> separate one.

> To make a unified composition on this basis it is
> necessary to find a composer whose views and methods
> are compatible with those of the choreographer. The
> composer who can overcome the limitations and problems

of dance accompaniment without sacrificing musical
form must possess a unique ingenuity and invention.

At the time of the writing of this article, Horton had
already coaxed musical scores out of two women, Bertha Miller
English and Constance Boynton. Within the next few years,
Dane Rudhyar and Sidney Cutner would compose numerous
works for the group. Before his association with Horton, Cutner
had written primarily for radio and films. Rudhyar was well
known in modern dance circles for his compositions as well as
for his fluent writings on art as propaganda.

Horton's outstanding collection of percussion instruments
played an important part in the creation of this new music.
What had started out as a random collection of Chinese and
Indian drums, picked up whenever Horton found one that he
could afford, was extended by a set of unmatched gamelan
pieces he had found in San Francisco. Also in the collection
were rattles; voodoo, Javanese, and Siamese drums; gongs from
Java, Indo-China, China, and Korea; water drums from the
South Seas; gamelan bells from the Philippines; a Kaffir piano
from South Africa; and temple bells, wood blocks, and fish
heads from China. These instruments were put to frequent use
in technique and composition classes as well as in scores for
concert pieces. Dancers in the group learned to play percussion
instruments as part of their training and were often called upon
to perform, both on the stage while dancing and in offstage
percussion orchestras.

The studio on Beverly Boulevard was fast becoming the
hub of modern dance activities on the West Coast, and lecture-
demonstrations and workshop performances were frequently
given for invited audiences. Chairs were set up at one end of
the extremely large room, and a theater atmosphere was approx-
imated as nearly as possible. A popular lecture Horton developed
was "The Function of the Dance in Acting," in which he

discussed his belief that an actor's movement was at least as important in communication as his spoken words. Dance, he believed, was an excellent discipline to liberate the innate physical expressiveness of the stage actor. He had proven this to his own satisfaction in his two prize-winning directorial efforts and was able to use practical illustrations to emphasize his points. Most often, however, the subject of the lecture-demonstration was the content of modern dance. A typical announcement promised a discussion of "Compositional Factors; Changing Technic, Technic and Creative Gymnastics, Content Dictates Form; and Musical Approach."

The demonstrations were well received, but they seemed to have neither the authority of his classroom teaching nor the dynamic impact of his concert work. Horton was not at his best when he was expounding intellectually. His brilliance was at the intuitive level, and though his manner when he narrated was warm and unassuming, from all accounts what was shown was much more exciting than what was said. Not surprisingly, dances which were evolved for lecture-demonstrations often turned out to be quite excellent and were later included in repertory. *Exhibition Dance No. 1,* one of his best pieces of this period, evolved from one of those demonstrations.

Horton's relatively sketchy background in the arts was a source of both weakness and strength. Never having been exposed to an integrated or sophisticated system from the point of view of a great school or teacher, he was continually searching, unconsciously perhaps, for the ingredients of an adequate foundation for his theorizing. Bella Lewitzky has said that his lack of theoretical knowledge was an advantage to him. "He would try anything or envision anything. Sometimes the shape of it would not be quite right but those who worked with him would help to shape it." The results were often naïve and incomplete, but with his growing maturity, more often they were stunning in their beauty, scope, and originality.

Sidney Cutner composed the music for the 1936 *Lysistrata*, which had its première at the Figueroa Playhouse with his wife, Ethel Nichols, dancing the title role and Bella Lewitzky as Myrrhina. This work was a further development of Horton's concept of the choreodrama, which had been launched with *Salome*. In this production the movement language was more abstract than it had been in *Salome* at the Shrine, and Horton showed signs of his growth as an artist by foregoing the use of large groups on stage to score choreographic points. The work was well received and in some performances brought cheers.

A pattern in newspaper criticism began to emerge which would sometimes amuse Horton but more often amaze him. Of the same work seen at the same performance, one critic wrote, "What the dances still need is more meaning for the layman," while another wrote, "It is a style of dance interpretation which Americans can understand and enjoy." Such contradictions were particularly common in the Los Angeles press during the 1930s. One thing that they all seemed to agree on was that although the work needed tightening in form, it was enjoyable and getting better with each concert. The criticisms were sometimes helpful but a far cry from the caliber of professional evaluation Horton needed during that important period. What was missing was the kind of feedback that could be expected from a discerning observer who could see his work in terms of his development as an artist as well as in the perspective of the development of modern dance in America. There simply was no one of the caliber of John Martin on the West Coast to provide the kind of knowledgeable criticism so essential to the development of an artist. Horton realized this, and years later did the only thing he could to get this kind of evaluation of his work: at his own expense he transported the group to New York to be seen by the best critics of his day.

Nineteen thirty-seven was a year full of excitement and fulfillment for Horton and his group. For several years they had been regarded by professional managers as a fine local organization but not one that would rank with the New York modern dance companies. Horton had fought against this attitude by producing consistently excellent work. Now the group was beginning to be regarded as professional and was represented by professional agents. Any lingering doubt about the group's ability had been dispelled by the work *Chronicle*, which led to unqualified praise and predictions of greater things to come. *Chronicle* was an iconoclastic saga dealing with the development of America in critical, yet positive, terms. The extensive program notes read:

> *Chronicle* is a record of the forces and trends of American society. Colonial Theme resolves into the imperialist forces which led to the opening of the new lands in America (Aggression), the exploitation of subject peoples, the negroes, Indians and European bondservants (Bondage). The religious bigotry of the period is personified in a solo figure (Prelude) and the individual revolt against oppressive authoritarian discipline finds expression in Fanatical Action. The forces of colonial autonomy and imperial rule clash in diplomatic arrogance, religious dissension and military struggle (Conflict). In the second part, Horizon marks the awakening awareness of the new self-ruling Americans to the potentialities of their land. Agrarian Possession symbolizes the close unity the settlers feel with their soil. War Cry heralds the destruction of a decadent economy in the old South. The gloomy period of Reconstruction opens with a dance of Mourning and ends with the vicious Incitation reminiscent of the unlawful Klan.

Salome, 1934;
Bruce Burroughs, Joy Montaya,
Elizabeth Talbot-Martin.
(Photo by Toyo Miyatake.)

Flight From Reality, 1937;
Lester Horton.
(Photo by
Viktor von Pribosic.)

Sacre du Printemps,
Rehearsal, 1937;
Bella Lewitzky.
(Photo by Leo Salkin.)

Sacre du Printemps,
Rehearsal, 1937;
Renaldo Alarcon.
(Photo by
Viktor von Pribosic.)

The section called "Incitation," later performed as "Terror, Ku Klux Klan," evolved with each performance. The night before a major Philharmonic Auditorium presentation, Horton re-choreographed the entire piece from beginning to end with a different viewpoint. This final version was the expression he had been seeking. Bella Lewitzky describes the performance:

> In 'Ku Klux Klan' I was the victim. (I was always the victim in Lester's work.) Because his love and regard for minority people would never permit anything like a black face, I wore brown, and had a brown veil over my head. I was completely covered by my costume—a total brown shape. The other shapes were red, but their faces and hands were free.
>
> The scene opened as four men carried me on their shoulders on a run across the stage. When they got me to the center, the act of incitation began with a group pattern of accusations, mounting to enormous fury. At the end, I had a series of escape runs. With each, somebody would catch me and push me back. At the very last moment, somebody caught my hand and pinned me in space, and all the figures were stilled as I swung from that hand. The curtain went down and then up again, and there was silence. We thought, 'Oh, you know, it was a turkey.' Then came a deafening roar as the whole house stood up. What had preceded was that once-in-a-while vacuum which occurs while an audience is absorbing a deep experience.

The only flaw in *Chronicle*, which was by all accounts a beautifully realized work, was the title. Martha Graham had first used it the month before. From time to time Horton would stumble across a title that particularly appealed to him and he would adopt it, apparently quite regardless of the fact that it had first been used by someone else. Much to the vexation of his colleagues, when they brought this "borrowing" to his attention, he shrugged it off with some annoyance. The work bore no resemblance to Graham's piece, which dealt with the Spanish Civil War, and he saw no reason to retitle it.

There was, however, an excellent reason. Impresario Merle Armitage had invited Horton to participate in a series of concerts at the Philharmonic Auditorium, which was to include the Graham and Humphrey-Weidman groups. Miss Graham had planned to show her *Chronicle* but graciously withdrew her piece and substituted another.

Frank Eng has said that Horton sometimes saw property ownership as a relative rather than an absolute concept. His years of legendary generosity more than prove how unimportant material ownership was to him. His food, his money, his clothing, his studio home and his classes were shared whenever a need was recognized. Whether or not this helps to explain Horton's propensity to borrow titles, we know that he damaged himself by his actions, partially obscuring for many years the quality and scope of his own gifts in the eyes of his East Coast colleagues.

Only Margaret Lloyd was able to see the whole picture clearly enough to say in the *Borzoi Book of Modern Dance*: "In the general conceptual exchange there is as much reason to suppose that the Eastern dancers picked up an idea or so from him as that he did all the borrowing." She points out, for example, that the "Agrarian Possession" section of *Chronicle* "showed a pioneer man and woman establishing their home amid the congratulatory celebration of their fellows—the very subject, though handled differently, of Martha Graham's much later *Appalachian Spring*." Lloyd also points out that Horton was using props, masks, and mobile architectural units and objects before Martha Graham had adopted functional decor for her theater pieces. She defends Horton by saying:

> There is some interrelation of influences, but each leader works primarily alone, and all work from the heritage

of what has gone before. The modern dance is not a
personal property but an open field. The motor laws
governing expressive body movement were established
long before they were perceived and adapted by the
creative modern dancer. The individual application of
these laws cannot help but vary, and the process of
individual discovery must inevitably continue.

It was, nevertheless, a sign of Horton's maturity that by
the late 1930s he gave up this obstinate borrowing which he had
done without so much as a "Please" or a "Thank you."

Chronicle took half an evening to perform. It was projected as a full-evening work but was never completed. Several
sections, including the highly successful "Terror, Ku Klux Klan,"
remained in his repertory.

Salome was revised for the Philharmonic presentation
with Bella Lewitzky dancing the title role, Horton the King, and
Kita van Cleve the Queen. With each successive revision of the
work the style and concept changed. Horton's inventive mind
could conceive movement almost faster than he or his dancers
could execute it, and when he redid *Salome* this time there was
little left of the previous version. His new version was a distinctly modern interpretation of the theme, and the roles of the
King and Queen were strengthened. The sensuality of Horton's
interpretation shocked W.E. Oliver into commenting in the *Los
Angeles Herald-Express*, "*Salome* is a remarkably theatrical
piece that goes just as far as possible on the public stage without
calling in the police." Helen W. King, more impressed by the
satire and theatricality of the piece, wrote in *Dance Magazine*:

> In the concluding number, a one-act choreodrama, *Salome*,
> the dancers managed to infuse something remarkably fresh
> considering the antiquity of the theme. It was satirical,
> clever, colorful and thoroughly delightful, well-costumed and
> furnished with exactly the right accompaniment through
> music composed for it by Bertha Miller English.

Horton injected a great deal of satirical humor into his
characterization of King Herod. Salome, danced by Bella
Lewitzky, came closer to my idea of what a Salome should
be than many a highly-touted dancer's work. The symbolism used in the portion of the dance where she receives
the head of John the Baptist was magnificently done.

The setting for *Salome* was an arrangement of large
geometric solids which had been contributed to the group by
Will Rogers, Jr., son of the famous cowboy philosopher. The
innovative lighting was designed so that shadows would emphasize
the planar differences between the shapes, causing the whole to
look like an enormous sculpture. Whenever the piece was
performed, Horton would carry paint and brushes to the theater,
and if the desired shadowing effect could not be achieved by the
available lighting he would touch up the set until he was
satisfied. Had the phrase been in use in 1937, the new *Salome*
would have been hailed as a "Total Theater" event.

Both Horton and William Bowne had become very
interested in the emotional and psychological connotations of
color; and the costumes and sets, which they worked on jointly,
explored a wide range of possibilities, using color from the
brightest to the dullest hues for symbolic effects. Less emphasis
was placed on shape of the costume during this period. Scarcely
a critic in the Los Angeles area failed to be impressed by the
brilliant effects achieved by this uninhibited use of color against
settings starkly etched by stage lighting. Isabel Morse Jones
praised the performers:

They are a dozen individualists with the true
ensemble feeling. They have discipline as well
as abandon. While the faces have the mask-look
of the modern intellectual there was a sensitive
rather than a hard quality about the set expression.

As a result of their growing popularity and acclaim, in August 1937 the Horton Dance Group was invited to dance Stravinsky's *Le Sacre du Printemps* at the enormous outdoor Hollywood Bowl. This was the first time the work would be staged on the West Coast, and the first anywhere by an American choreographer. The detailed scenario gives an interesting insight into Horton's approach to this ambitious undertaking. (For *Sacre* program notes, see page 215.) Costumes by William Bowne were in earth colors: brown, black, red, and white. Lewitzky's spectacular entrance as "The Chosen One" was on a bed of flowers held aloft by several dancers, and every element of color and shape was calculated to be set off by the pristine brightness of the enormous white Hollywood Bowl shell. Horton's years of exploration into the movement motifs of primitive peoples was excellent preparation for this undertaking; the movement style best suited to the work was actually built right into his training techniques. Excitement at the Beverly Boulevard studio was at fever pitch. Everyone was aware that Horton and Bowne were doing some of their finest work.

After months of grueling day and night rehearsals the cast, headed by Bella Lewitzky and Renaldo Alarcon, was not prepared for the crisis which greeted them at dress rehearsal. Efrem Kurtz, the conductor, announced that it was impossible for the Los Angeles Philharmonic to play the then unfamiliar piece with only the one scheduled rehearsal. Just as all seemed lost, the concert master, Henry Svedrofsky, informed Horton that he could pull the orchestra together for all of *Sacre* except the finale with one extra rehearsal. The cost of the extra rehearsal was $1000. The fee to Horton and the company for the entire production, including costumes, was $1000. They paid and performed the piece without the finale.

Like the Diaghilev Ballets Russes production in 1913, *Sacre* raised a storm of protest. There was shouting and cat-calling and people headed for the box office to demand refunds. The audience was startled by the harmonic and rhythmic excitement of the unfamiliar score, and by the angular and sensual movements of the dancers. Many had come to see a ballet. Not only were the performers barefoot, but their movements were unfamiliar, disturbing, and, to some, obscene. Some critics, however, felt otherwise:

> The modern realism, forthrightness and stark ugliness incorporated by the Horton Group suited the music. There was something close to the art-loving Mexican in its dance figures and the costumes. The colors were primitive, earthy and added interesting pattern to the choreography. The authentic ceremonial atmosphere was rigidly preserved by the dancers and this was occasionally misunderstood by the spectators for they tittered audibly. . . . Lester Horton's Ballet moved people to expression one way or the other. People either idealized its inspiration, its intellectuality or they railed at its grotesqueries. The company and conductor were tendered enthusiastic applause at its conclusion.

> One word describes the ballet Lester Horton created to the music of Stravinsky's *Le Sacre du Printemps*, and that word is: Exciting! It was one of the most exciting dance experiences I have had. . . . There are undoubtedly parts of this ballet which may well be strengthened, but taken as a whole, Stravinsky may well be happy that Horton has done justice to his *Rite of Spring*.

Sacre was being discussed in musical and artistic circles, and at last Horton was becoming known to a larger audience than the tiny modern dance public. The work was repeated in April of the following year at Royce Hall at the University of California, Los Angeles, without major incident. In addition to *Sacre*, the concert included *Chronicle*; *Pasaremos*, a piece dealing with the Spanish Civil War; and *Haven*, an interpretation of a frenzied religious service inspired by the Holy Rollers. For this production of *Sacre*, U.C.L.A. art instructor Warren Cheney designed duplications of towering Easter Island idols. The problem of accompaniment was more simply solved this time by using recordings, and the finale was reinstated for this performance.

A third major appearance of the Lester Horton Dance Group in 1937 was a joint recital with Michio Ito and Spanish dancer-choreographer, José Fernandez, at the Greek Theater in Los Angeles. Horton presented *Salome* and *Prologue to an Earth Celebration.* Ito's offerings included *Gnossiennes, Minuet,* and *Blue Danube Waltz* and Fernandez did *18th Century Spain* (from "Goyescas"), *Mexican Poem,* and *Garrotur* (Gypsy Dance). The performance was excellently reviewed, with the Horton group and Fernandez sharing most of the praise. Michio Ito, Horton's master of less than a decade before, suffered at the hands of the critics who felt that his material was old-fashioned. Once again Horton had felt the need to rework *Salome* completely. This time there was no doubt that he had surpassed himself and created what the critics apparently felt was a minor masterpiece:

> Lester Horton's choreo-drama with unusually inter-
> esting percussion by Bertha English, was *Salome.*
> This group is now an integral body of dancers with
> a single purpose. *Salome,* gruesome, decadent and
> impressive, has been intensified since its last
> performance here. The lighting was dramatic. . . .
> The company, including Horton as Herod, has
> perfected its interpretation to a point where there
> is little more possible.

Encouraged by their growing success, in the spring of 1938 the group decided to venture north and make their San Francisco debut. They presented, among other works, their

successful *Salome* at the Community Playhouse on April 24,
1938. The following day critic Alfred Frankenstein had this to
say:

> Eventually modern choreographers will cease to make
> obeisance to Graham and Holm, and the new dance will
> be really new. This was, indeed, suggested in the final
> offering of the program, a "choreo-drama" entitled
> *Salome*, in which the ancient Biblical story was given
> most exciting treatment, admirably combining both
> choreographic and pantomimic ideas. The piece was
> brutal and fast and fantastic as a modern *Salome* should
> be, and was altogether one of the most gripping theatrical
> versions of the tale it has been my privilege to see.

In the summer of 1938 Horton was invited to teach a
workshop production group at Mills College and to create a
new work for the student dancers. Bella Lewitzky was to
share teaching responsibliities and be co-choreographer. The
other workshop teacher for the summer session, Graham-trained
Bonnie Bird, was assisted by a gifted young man named Mercier
(later, Merce) Cunningham.

At Mills, Horton turned once more to Mexico's tempestuous past for a major work, *Conquest*. Mexico had become for
him a symbol of the struggle for social and economic justice.
The opening section of the piece told the legend of the god,
Quetzalcoatl, who introduced the arts to his people. The
"Spanish Conquest" followed, leading to a section titled
"Inquisition," in which Horton used the dancers' bodies both
as instruments of torture and as victims. The vain attempts to
fuse the Spanish and Aztec ways of life left a prophet carrying
the strength of rebellion into the final section, "Tierra y
Libertad!" Here Horton was at his theatrical and choreographic
best. The movements of the Spanish figures, typified by an

elegant carriage of the body and heavy leg lifts, were contrasted with the Mexicans' movements, which were close to the floor, employing complex rhythmical footwork. Imperceptibly at first, and then with growing strength, the Mexican theme drowned out the Spanish theme, and at the climax Lewitzky, as the "Spirit of the People," made her entrance. She appeared at the top of an offstage ramp and advanced toward the audience beating a compelling foot pattern of six beats against nine. The people triumphed! The audience cheered at each performance. Horton had become a master of his craft.

Conquest was a perfect vehicle for Horton. He was able to combine his fascination with folklore, his interest in ethnic forms, and his desire to make a pertinent statement of social significance in one effort. He was a great admirer of the Mexican artists, Orozco, Sequeiros, and Rivera; and the colors and shapes of the country's folk art had captivated him from his earliest years in California.

The principal parts in Conquest were taken by Bella Lewitzky and Merce Cunningham. James Lyons, June Fulton, Dorothy Gillanders, and Dorothy Herman were also featured. Thirty-five years later Cunningham recalled choreographic sessions in which Horton, seated in a chair and smoking a cigar, would somehow design ingenious lifts and how Lewitzky bounded off into space at the slightest suggestion from the choreographer.

Composer Lou Harrison, who has since created many distinguished scores for modern dance, found Horton to be an ideal co-worker:

> I was much influenced by Lester, his magic stimulus,
> imagination, humor and general loveliness. Certainly he
> was much ahead (present theater developments are
> closer to him than ever) and working with him was
> always exciting. . . . It was Lester who "full-scale"
> alerted me to the glories of Mexico as "folk-culture"

and "classical ancient culture." Through his own singing
I first heard La Sandunga and many other such melodies.
(For complete letter, see page 232.)

For his instrumentation of *Conquest* Harrison used piano,
flute, a conch shell, a "thunder sheet," and flower pots which he
filled with varying amounts of water. When struck, the pots
made a gamelan-like sound. The device later appeared in his
work, *Song of Quetzalcoatl*. Intrigued by Horton's ideas about
integrated production, the talented and enthusiastic young
musician also worked with him on the decor for *Conquest*.

Horton's propensity for re-working his own pieces,
changing titles and composers, may be illustrated by comparing
Conquest with *Tierra y Libertad!*, the same piece renamed and
presented at the Philharmonic Auditorium in 1939. The
"Celebration" section appears on some of the programs, but
not all. Public and critics alike were sometimes confused, not
to mention the dancers, who were not quite sure until the last
possible minute which version would be decided upon. Bella
Lewitzky recalls chasing after Horton before one major
performance, program in hand, trying to find out which dance
was which. With his own sometimes peculiar brand of logic
Horton saw no oddity in this. His performers had to keep constantly "tuned in" to be sure which of two, three, or more
versions he was calling for at any given time.

In 1939 we find Horton again employing the lecture-
demonstration form. In February he hired the 1,294 seat
Wilshire-Ebell Theater to present *Introduction to the Dance*.
Part I demonstrated "Technics in compositional form and
studies in turns, falls, and dimensional springs." Part II
illustrated "Dance Construction," and Part III consisted of
three works from the repertory. A highlight was *Departure
From the Land*, a moving evocation of the Dust Bowl emigration
predating the publication of John Steinbeck's *The Grapes of Wrath*

by a few months. Music for the entire program was composed by
Gerhardt Dorn, musical director for the group, and the art
direction was under Robert Tyler Lee, who was to become a well-
known designer for television.

For several months the performing group was idle, with
Horton apparently concentrating on the development of the
"School of the Horton Dance Group." Technique and choreography classes were expanded. A Christmas course was initiated,
and greater attention was being given to the children's classes under
the supervision of company member Jeri Faubion (Salkin). She
later confided that Horton had declared her expert in this field a
little before the fact and that she nearly developed ulcers living
up to his claims. His faith, however, had been well placed. She
became an excellent teacher of children in record time. Years
later she was to become a pioneer worker in the field of dance
therapy, using her Horton training as a basis for the work which
she describes in her book *Body Ego Technique*.*

Her future husband, Leo Salkin, took some of the finest
photos of the company during those years, prompted partly by
Horton's need for his skills and partly by Horton's faith in his
ability to do the job well. They seemed instinctively to understand one another and the results were seen in some inspired
photography, including memorable candid shots of the choreographer relaxing away from his studio. Such events were not
considered unique. One only wondered which hidden talents
Horton would uncover when an unsuspecting friend or husband
started hanging around the group. The word "charisma" was not
in popular usage then, and Horton was too democratic in his
dealings to be called inspiring. People routinely accepted these
miracles and said, "That's Lester!"

The handsome school brochure, dated September 12, 1938
through June 9, 1939, includes an interesting statement of

*Jeri Salkin, *Body Ego Technique* (Springfield, Illinois: C.C. Thomas 1973).

objectives for the "Youth Program," indicating Horton's advanced
concepts of teaching children at this time:

> OBJECTIVES: To stimulate the imagination and develop
> creative attitudes; to inculcate recognition of the body
> capacities and to develop mastery of the body as an
> instrument of social expression. The courses are designed
> for various age levels—but all are constructed on the same
> basis. The classes are composed of technic, elements of
> music and dance creation. The creative program is
> augmented by formal dances, (technical pieces to develop
> skill and design in movement), folk dance, (Mexican—
> Indian—Hungarian—etc.), to instill an appreciation of other
> cultures, period dances, (the dance forms which preceed
> the ballet—such as the sarabande, pavane, minuet, etc.
> These dances are emphasized because of their effect upon
> musical development and reflection of social history.)

Horton believed that his own exploration of ethnic dance
had not only broadened his knowledge and appreciation of the
varieties of human movement but had taught him, as well, a
profound respect for the similarities and differences that exist
among all people everywhere. He wished to pass this along to the
youngsters who studied in his school.

His training techniques were developing rapidly in both
depth and objectivity. Pelvic movements from African origins
were increasingly important; second and fourth positions continued to be emphasized, and a great deal of time was spent on
exercises developed from swinging movements. Rib articulations
were sharp, clear, and exact. Slow movements were to be
executed almost imperceptibly, as in Japanese theater dance. The
fast movements and elevations were always a breath beyond
attainment so that the dancers were continually being challenged.
Paradoxically, notwithstanding its masculine sweep and grandeur,
the Horton training was emerging as an essentially lyrical technique.

If one identifying feature of a Horton-trained dancer were to be described, it would be extraordinary fluidity of movement.

An ever present theme in Horton's teaching was the importance of nourishing the imaginative capacities of his dancers, a fact remembered with appreciation by many who spent their formative years with him. This interest is reflected in an article Horton wrote for *Educational Dance Magazine* in 1940 on the teaching of composition.

> Every teacher, (every dancer, indeed) is familiar with the utter inadequacy the student feels when he is asked to invent movement. Anyone with decent humility is sure to be confounded by the request. When the problem is to improvise, the reaction is still more general and pronounced. And how this reaction impedes growth in the dance composer! Free fantasy is a priceless attribute which we sell in exchange for a stodgy education during our childhood. Imagination is exchanged for rationality. We need them both to compose. The gift for fantasy, for a free invention of movement, must be regained. (See page 202.)

So great was his respect for individuality that he had no interest in training his dancers to develop a distinctively Horton "look." It was enough that they be responsive, strong, and versatile. Horton-trained people later won easy acceptance by such varied choreographers as Glen Tetley, Agnes de Mille, John Butler, Martha Graham, and Jerome Robbins.

Although he was eminently successful in developing spontaneous expressiveness in his dancers, Horton fared less well in composition classes. Because new movement ideas came to him so easily, he did not *need* his dancers' choreographic skills in the same way that he needed their dance or theater production skills, and his teaching here, though sound, was not particularly inspiring. He himself often grappled unsuccessfully with problems of form, and his attenuated works were saved only by theatricality or moments so choreographically potent that they helped to obscure his shortcomings. In his attempts to evolve a sequence of learning related to composition which would satisfy him—and he tried several—he came upon the idea of having his students study three-dimensional form in great art works as well as create their own original plastic forms in clay and wood. It was an exciting and organic way of broadening their perceptiveness about art, at the same time illustrating his intense belief that all people are capable of success in some form of creative activity.

In the late 1930s several dancers in the group were singled out for special praise by the press. Eleanor Brooks came into her own during this period and danced several lead parts. Her brooding and earthy intensity was a good contrast to Bella Lewitzky's agile, almost athletic bravura dancing. Jeri Faubion, Patricia McGrath, and Kita van Cleve were also frequently mentioned.

Several young male dancers were attracted to the school and company by the excitement and creativity. Maurice Bailey, Herman Boden, David Lober, James Mitchell, Newell Reynolds, and Leon Rapoport (Paul Steffen) made their first appearances as Horton dancers in the late thirties and early forties. Brahm van den Berg, still an impressive performer, rejoined the company for a while.

On November 3, 1939, The Horton Dance Group made its last major appearance at the Philharmonic Auditorium, once again inaugurating a dance series for impresario Merle Armitage. The series included Lincoln Kirstein's *Ballet Caravan*, and among the dancers were Harald Kreutzberg, Hanya Holm, Martha Graham, Carmelita Maracci, and Angna Enters.

In addition to *Tierra y Libertad!*, Horton debuted a new catchall revue format, *Something to Please Everybody*, which he was to utilize for several seasons with characteristic deletions, additions and changes of title. (See page 221.) For this first version he included a few works done previously and several new, lighter pieces. On November 5, W. E. Oliver wrote the following in the *Los Angeles Herald-Express:*

> Although this part of the evening's work was turned over to the more popular side of dancing, there was no let down in technic and finish of production. In fact, these dozen short items represent the most polished efforts the Horton Group have gathered in one concert.
>
> Scaling the extraordinary gamut of technic that the Horton style of dancing permits, this first half of the program included such varied items as "Pathos", danced by three girls in perfect choreography; "Narrative", a sprightly paraphrase of the conventional ballet; "Oriental", Lester Horton's annual caricature of the androgynous rumors attached to the dance cult; "Aphrodisiac", a playful fiddling with the strip tease idea; "Surrealism", healthy fun with the screwball side of art; "Primitive" . . . [and] "Romantic Duo", an exquisite version of boy tenderly meeting girl.

An account of Horton's own performance in "Oriental" suggests that he had not lost his satiric gifts during several years of producing message dances.

> Blossoming out in flowering yellow, purple, green, blue, and orange costume, Lester Horton delighted his Philharmonic audiences last Friday night with an exceedingly droll and humorous take-off on the Oriental dance. His wiggling toes, fluttering fingers, and poker face accompanied by a gaping mouth called for repeated curtain calls.

A few more paragraphs from the same review give us a delightful picture of Horton's versatility and showmanship.

> Marching out onto the stage in pairs, attired in simple white silk skirts, blouses, and slacks, the 16 young men and women were introduced by Horton with mute gestures augmented by a concealed narrator, who also explained the rest of the program as it unfolded . . .

> Curtain calls were taken in the peculiar mood of the dance they followed, and only made the audience doubly enthusiastic. The sleep walker of the Surrealism number was still walking during the first curtain call, but at the last one she had worked up to a running gait.

In several of these pieces Horton experimented with levels, flat forms, and three-dimensional props and sets. Dancers manipulated screens in "Surrealism," allowing only their hands and feet to be seen. The main set piece was a Calder-like assemblage with Daliesque hands hanging from strings. The sparse set, designed by William Bowne for *Departure from the Land*, was made up of slim wood battens designed to give the skeletal impression of a prairie homestead. He anticipated the use of these scenic ideas on the East Coast by several years.

The nearly sold-out house cheered the evening from the beginning. Five years of artistic productivity on the part of the Horton Dance Group had been significant in the creation of a large and loving audience for dance in Los Angeles, a fact remarked on by many critics. Merle Armitage was moved to make an unprecedented curtain speech during intermission, in which he praised the contributions of the Horton Dance Group to the cultural life of the city.

Among the enthusiastic viewers at this concert, according to Isabel Morse Jones in her rave review in the *Los Angeles*

Times, were hundreds of Disney Studios animators. The dance-filled *Fantasia* with a spectacular *Rite of Spring* section was then in preparation. Jones concluded her article with:

> The Horton Dance Group deserves place with the leading
> creative dancers of the country. With persistence and
> devotion, Lester Horton has produced Western American
> art form in the dance through years of sacrifice. His
> dancers have a distinctive technique, and the strength
> and precision of trained acrobats with which to present
> a repertoire that interests the theater public and the
> modern art intellectual.

The next problem was: Where to go from here? Everyone had ideas but no one seemed to be able to offer the wherewithal.

A theme that was appearing with increasing frequency in reviews of the Horton Dance Group was that the time was ripe for a presentation in New York City, the capital of the American dance world. For a while Sol Hurok expressed interest in arranging a tour, but the venture would have required Horton to make a substantial cash outlay, and there simply was no money. The Dance Group had only recently reached a point where it was breaking even at the box office.

A few years earlier there had been a vague possibility of a European tour for the company and *Dance Magazine* writer Helen King, who believed Horton ranked with the finest in modern dance, had written a two-page article titled "Show America First." Horton would have been happy to. He was to be frustrated time after time in his attempts to secure bookings for a cross-country tour and for tours abroad. Working as he did with a relatively large group, he had a fairly expensive attraction; but the real problem was that impresarios, whose success had traditionally been with dancers from Europe and New York, were reluctant to take a chance on a California group.

Horton's sweeping sagas of the late 1930s and the style
in which they were performed would have made good propaganda abroad, had a tour ever materialized. There was an
aggressive masculinity to his work in both the choreographic
material and the sometimes brash and clumsy but always extro-
verted movement vocabulary. This was a statement of health,
for Horton had not yet lost touch with his basic innocence and
he was incurably optimistic. His own openness and vulnerability,
which were so appealing in his personality, were reflected in the
work and the way he spoke about it:

> We are trying to create a dance expression which is
> truly American . . . We feel we are making progress but
> the whole thing is in a state of evolvement. We con-
> stantly change. We have discarded what we did last
> year, although we thought it good. Next year we may
> retain little of this year's work. That is the way we
> grow. There can be nothing static about our work if we
> are to succeed.

In 1939 Horton was invited by Mary Jane Hungerford to
teach a summer workshop at the University of Southern California, and the following year he returned to Mills College, this
time with full company. Again with Lou Harrison composing,
he presented *Something to Please Everybody* and *Sixteen to
Twenty-Four*, which dealt with America's urban problems. The
sections were titled: "Birthright," "Problems—Men and Women
Without Work, Deferred Marriage, Threat of War," and "Resolve."
The piece was done in the manner of a documentary film,
accompanied by a running narrative with the dancers themselves
interjecting exclamatory phrases. The subject matter of the new
dance marked a departure for Horton. Until this time his
themes had ranged from the ethnic, through social injustice and

anti-Fascist pieces, to the sweeping themes of American and
Mexican history. Now he was looking at the individual affected
by his immediate environment, and expressing concern for a
generation that had been tortured by a depression and was now
facing the inevitability of a great war. The work did not fare
well. It was somewhat self-conscious and not well timed.
(Newell Reynolds has characterized it as "agit prop with a
sledge hammer.") In response to their vocal plea for jobs, the
dancers received suggestions in the mail as to where work was
available. The piece was abandoned after a few more presentations.

Occasional mishaps notwithstanding, the group was
growing in popularity, and with plaudits coming in on all sides
they continued to perform frequently. In November, 1940, at
the Wilshire-Ebell Theater, *Lysistrata* was revived as *A Noble
Comedy*. Horton devised some of his most interesting and
elaborate choreography to date in telling a fragment of the
story of the rebellion of women of ancient Greece against their
war-minded men. A few months later, when the work was
repeated at the Hollywood Music Box Theater, Viola Swisher,
earlier one of his severest critics, was moved to unrestrained
praise. Writing in the *Hollywood Citizen News* on February 3,
1941, she placed the company indisputably in the top ranks
among dance modernists, noting that in the three-month
interval from the Ebell performance, both the choreographies
and their execution had been notably tightened and polished.

> With the same keen efficiency that is to be found in
> fine line drawings, Horton has created choreographies
> alive with vitality, purpose and legitimate artistic com-
> pulsion. And let there be no mistake about this: He
> created—not copied—all the way . . . "Noble Comedy,"
> the Lysistrata story again, danced to music by Simon
> Abel, showed Horton's increasing mastery of form and

composition in the realm of the full-length ballet. Its
persuasive humor and interesting action were well
emphasized throughout.

As its popularity grew, the group adopted once again the
name of Horton Ballets for the 1942 season.   Performances at
the Saturday Morning Musical Club, the Wilshire-Ebell, and a
return engagement at Royce Hall, U.C.L.A. featured *Tierra y
Libertad!*, and *Something to Please Everybody*, the latter now
with music by Lou Harrison, Sidney Cutner, Heitor Villa Lobos,
Domingo Santa Cruz, Jacques Press, Raymond Scott, and Dimitri
Shostakovitch. Choreographically, however, Horton seemed to
have reached a fallow period, concentrating primarily on
strengthening and revising these two earlier pieces.

In *Something to Please Everybody*, there had been a
conscious shifting to attractiveness—an expressed longing to
produce, at last, works for which pay for the dancers was even
conceivable. The opportunities came quickly. Within months
the group was working simultaneously at the Orpheum Theater
in downtown Los Angeles (four performances a day), rehearsing
for Horton's first motion picture assignment for Universal
International Studios, *Moonlight in Havana,* and preparing for
a concert. The schedule was backbreaking, but for the first
time the Lester Horton dancers were salaried.

In 1943 three film assignments came through from the
same studio. Horton's background was ideal for the "exotic"
films which were their speciality. He choreographed *Rhythm of
the Islands*, *White Savage*, and the more sedate *Phantom of the
Opera* with Claude Rains and Susanna Foster. The dancers also
made an appearance at Earl Carroll's then world-famous supper
club to excellent reviews. Herman Boden, who had worked
closely with Horton during those years, commented in 1970:

Everyone loved to work for Lester in films. Other
choreographers were still working pretty much as they

Idea Session, 1941;
Bella Lewitzky,
Newell Reynolds,
Eleanor Brooks,
James Mitchell,
Lester Horton,
Maurice Bailey,
Kita van Kleve.
(Photo by Leo Salkin.)

Production
Preparations, 1941;
James Mitchell,
William Bowne,
Leon Rapaport,
Maurice Bailey,
Herman Boden.
(Dance Theater
Collection.)

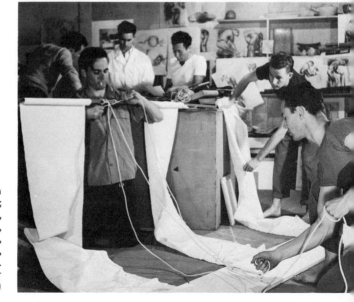

Bella Lewitzky, James Mitchell, 1942.
(Photo by Tom Binford.)

had in the 1930s. Hermes Pan was basically a "hoofer,"
and Albertina Rasch was doing ballet. Lester did
careful research; even on the low budget films he
attempted to bring some quality to the work. Often
as not the finished film showed close-ups of Maria Montez
or Yvonne de Carlo—whoever the exotic lady happened
to be—and not much of our work. We did the difficult
material in the background and much of that ended up
on the cutting room floor. Lester was not discouraged,
and we would all work even harder on the next one. He
was ahead of his time, trying to do that kind of quality
work in films.

At this point the personnel of the company sustained
serious losses. Several of the male dancers were drafted, while
others were lured away by the salaries offered by show business
or by the burgeoning wartime economy. Horton was at a
creative impasse, and he became restless and depressed.
Exhausted by the years of struggle at near poverty level, he
accepted an offer to take his group to New York to perform for
the opening of a lavish nightclub, the Folies Bergère, in the hope
that keeping the group employed would hold them together for
concert work. It was also an opportunity to work in New York,
and under any circumstances that sounded good to him in 1943.

 interlude

When Horton arrived in New York, the problems that
were thrust at the unsuspecting choreographer bordered on the
sinister, according to his letter to Katherine Stubergh a few
months later. Intrigues, some of which he never quite
comprehended, were rife. The European representatives of the
venture seemed to be continually shouting at each other in
French, German, and Italian, none of which Horton understood.
Soon they were shouting at him as well. They were not happy
with his ideas as translated for them by interpreters. What they
wanted from him, he felt, would have worked well in Paris in
1922. He would not concede. To worsen the situation, the
California dancers arrived on the scene angry and irritable due to
misunderstandings, all of which they felt were Horton's fault.
Tempers flared. The Folies management threatened litigation and
the Union, the American Guild of Variety Artists, was brought
in to calm the dancers, but to little avail. Matters worsened as
the shouting continued. A few company members were in open
revolt. The situation had all of the improbability and none of
the humor of a 1930s musical farce.

Horton was ill-equipped by experience or inclination to
battle his way out of the messy situation. A few times, when
he had reached his limit of tolerance, he disappeared for a
while, much to everyone's amazement and chagrin. He would

reappear whenever he felt he could handle more bickering and shouting.

Some relief came with the arrival of the dancer Sonia Shaw and her wealthy husband, William Katzell. After sizing up the situation, Katzell dispatched his attorney to look into the Folies morass, and within a few days what had appeared to be hopelessly confused problems were straightened out with the management. The dancers, however, continued to fume. A few weeks later, the Katzells made Horton an alluring proposal. Miss Shaw, who had worked with Horton in Los Angeles and recognized his enormous talent, wished to pursue a career in modern dance. Her husband, who was seriously interested in theatrical production, was willing to provide financial backing for a company which would tour internationally, using Horton's works as the foundation of the repertoire. There was also some talk of producing a musical later with Horton as the choreographer.

Shaw had chosen both wisely and well. Of all the top-ranking choreographers in the modern field at the time, Horton was the only one whose entire choreographic energy went into creating roles for other dancers. By dancing for him, she would stand a good chance of being catapulted to the first ranks of the profession. Time was needed to work out the details of the plan. The Katzells promised to contact Horton when they were ready.

When the Folies Bergère finally opened, it was a huge success. There were rave notices from the entertainment critics for the dancers and the brilliant young comedienne, Imogene Coca, one of the headliners of the show. However, one reviewer was decidedly not impressed. The respected dance critic, Edwin Denby, had come to see the work of the renowned West Coast choreographer and was dismayed at the production, which featured brassy costumes and an almost psychedelic mirrored set. He wrote a short but harsh review expressing his "complete disappointment."

What Horton had given the Folies was exaggeratedly flashy and eagerly devoured by entertainment-hungry wartime audiences, but certainly not art. *Boogie Bali Woogie, Embolada, African Drum Dance,* and *Victory Ball Waltz* were performed by the company with typical Horton style and polish. Offers of work poured in, including two from the prestigious William Morris agency, but Horton was too exhausted to consider staying on in a New York which had become a nightmare.

The Folies experience had been hard on the morale of the group. They had been trained to be concert performers and loathed competing with the sounds of a crowded, noisy supper club. At the end of the run several decided to go their separate ways, and Horton had no choice but to disband the group. For the first time in over ten years of uninterrupted creative achievement there were no longer any Lester Horton Dancers. Many times during the next ten years Horton would stubbornly try to hold his groups together by getting commercial employment for them, but the results were repeatedly frustrating. He would gain a little extra time with them for his concert work, and after a while perhaps that was all he ever hoped for. The process was extremely painful, but he courageously became an expert at "starting again."

After the Folies job was finished, Horton and Bella Lewitzky resumed teaching at the Beverly Boulevard studio. For several months as well Horton worked on Universal International's film *Climax.* He waited for the Katzells to contact him, eager and impatient to return to concert work. When he finally heard from them, there was a painful stipulation in their proposal: Bella was not to be included in the venture. Shaw wished no competition. Horton agreed. The opportunity to work, at last, with adequate financial backing and the possibility that his work would be seen in New York as well as abroad were greater temptations than he could resist, regardless of his moral obligation to Lewitzky.

The apparent ease with which Horton accepted the terms
of the agreement left a scar on the relationship with his lead
dancer and collaborator which would never fully heal. It was one
of the few drastic compromises Horton made in his career and
one he was to regret. Lewitzky, in the prime of her early
performing career, had been working and building with him for
nearly a decade. She felt hurt and quietly but deeply resented
his acceptance of these terms. Eventually she forgave him but
she did not forget. When Horton left for his new assignment, she
stayed on to teach at the school with William Bowne.

After a solid two months of auditioning in New York,
the new company was selected. In addition to Shaw, the dancers
were Alice Dudley, Malka Farber, Saida Gerrard, Peggy Holmes,
and Betty Lind. The gentlemen were Richard D'Arcy and James
Mitchell, the only dancer involved from the old group. The little
company moved up to a defunct boys' camp in the vicinity of
Bennington, Vermont, and *Tierra Y Libertad!* and *Something to
Please Everybody* went into rehearsal. In the Horton tradition
the group worked morning, noon, and night. After a two-and-a-
half-hour morning warm-up they rehearsed continually till ten at
night, stopping only for meals and very brief rest periods. Horton
seemed to be trying harder than ever to make the venture work,
and Saida Gerrard remembers that the dancers would joke that
he sometimes considered as many as fourteen versions of one
twelve-count phrase before he would choose one. She nicknamed
him "Penelope," after the wife of Odysseus, who wove all day
and unraveled what she had done every night. After four or five
weeks nothing was completed, but apparently no one was very
upset by that, since the movement style was interesting and
challenging for the young dancers and enthusiasm was running
high. Then, as fate would have it, Shaw injured her knee, and
at about the same time her husband began to find the venture
more expensive than he had anticipated. He felt compelled to

withdraw his support and the undertaking, so filled with promise, was called off.

Horton was stunned by the sudden collapse of the project and spent several weeks at the Vermont camp resting and trying to get his bearings. Just as he had not quite understood Lewitzky's distress with his taking an assignment which deliberately excluded her, now he could not bring himself to see the unfairness of Katzell's action. Somehow he had learned to believe the best of people, and once he accepted someone as a friend the evidence had to be crushing before he would give up staunchly defending him. Horton had blind spots. Sometimes, as with Bella Lewitzky, they caused pain to people who trusted him, but more often, as in this case, he was his own victim.

When Horton had recovered sufficiently, he and James Mitchell, who had stayed behind with him, stopped in New York to spend a few days before leaving for California. Mitchell heard of a dance call for a new Harold Arlen musical and, encouraged by Horton, went to his first audition for the experience. When it was over, the choreographer, Agnes de Mille, of *Oklahoma!* and *Carousel* fame, called him over and asked where he had gotten his training. When he told her that he had worked with Horton and Lewitzky, de Mille, who knew their teaching, said, "The job is yours." The job was the dance lead in *Bloomer Girl*, and his first of many important Broadway dance and acting roles, including the creation of the role of Harry Beaton in *Brigadoon*. Mitchell was to go on to a successful career in motion pictures and television.

Mitchell recalled that when Horton, himself nearly penniless, embarked for California, he overlooked packing a considerable number of clothing essentials, knowing that the young dancer after five years of concert work had literally nothing to his name. It was a typical Horton gesture; knowing when and how his help was needed, he gave generously and inconspicuously.

Horton returned to Los Angeles once again, this time to work under contract to Universal International Studios on the films *That Night With You, Frisco Sal, Shady Lady,* and *Salome, Where She Danced.* In yet another attempt to find paying work for dancers which would make it possible for them to continue their concert work, he conceived the idea of a series of short dance feature films which could be filmed inexpensively using unknown talent (his dancers) and all original choreography. The project was called "Dancing Americans." The subject matter covered a wide range of ideas from a whodunit mystery to a Mexican Fiesta featuring authentic folk dances. The choreographer's flair for satiric humor is seen in several of the delightful outlines which he presented, complete with shooting scripts, to producers at Universal International Studios. *Dilly Dali* for example:

> The story of a lonely secretary to an art dealer who encounters Surrealism, unleashing a surge of urges, mostly libidinous — so wacky as to circumvent the need for censorship. Underlying this action are many jibes at Surrealists who are not mysteries to any ticket purchaser over the age of nine.

The proposal was not accepted, but it is interesting to note how Horton's belief that a film concentrating on dance could be commercially successful anticipated the popularity of *The Red Shoes* and *The Tales of Hoffman* by several years.

Suddenly, with no warning Poly Anna and Iredell Horton announced their intention of moving to California to be with Lester. Horton had made the mistake of urging his parents to see a few of the films he had worked on. Having seen them, they somehow assumed that their son must be doing very well financially and could afford to look after them a bit. Actually, his net income that year from the Katzell venture and film work was only a little over $5,000, and much of this went to repay old debts.

Horton scarcely had time to warn his parents that they would have to share living space in the studio. Poly Anna was miserable from the day she arrived. She was confused by the activities of the studio and intimidated by the high-spirited young dancers who were always coming and going. A few trips around the Hollywood area convinced her that she hated it and she stubbornly refused to set foot outside the building. Iredell adapted better to the new surroundings and not only did the family shopping but made himself useful doing odd jobs. They are remembered as a querulous home-spun couple with little warmth for anyone but their son and Bill Bowne.

In 1944 Horton seriously injured his neck while making repairs in the studio. His larynx was affected, and for a while he could barely speak. The injury resulted in some loss of mobility, but the posture he adopted to control the discomfort added to his already regal and impressive bearing.

Some months later, when the Beverly Boulevard Studio was sold and the dancers were asked to move, Horton and Bowne bought a house in the sun-drenched, rocky Chatsworth area of the San Fernando Valley. It was to be home for Lester's parents and a weekend retreat for Lester and Bill. The old couple took to the place immediately. They planted an ambitious garden and raised rabbits for eating. Iredell built ingenious quarters for the snakes and alligator which Bill and Lester kept as pets. Horton's interest in herpetology remained undiminished during his lifetime.

The parting with William Katzell in 1944 must somehow have been settled amicably, for late in 1945, when Katzell bought the rights to produce a musical, *Shootin' Star,* based on the life of Billy the Kid, he invited Horton to do the choreography. The dancers selected in New York for the production were excellent. Many of them were on the threshold of

important careers in modern dance and ballet. Some familiar
names from the out-of-town program are Nelle Fisher, Ray
Harrison, Francisco Moncion, Herbert Ross, Doris Ebener
(Rudko), Nona Shurman, Billie Kirpich, Lavina Nielson, Edythe
Udane, and, of course, Sonia Shaw. Nathan Kirkpatrick and
Sonia Shaw had featured roles.

Shootin' Star had a major strike against it from the
beginning: a weak book. The production had been conceived as
a lyric drama, with both drama and music flowing into the
action of the play. Production numbers and ballets were to be
avoided as potential show stoppers. Horton understood, for he
had been working on his own concept of integrated theater for
many years. The cast was enthusiastic about the score and the
singing voice of a then unknown talent, Doretta Morrow. David
Brooks, Howard da Silva, Bernice Parks, and Susan Reed were
starred. Everyone was hoping that the first-rate cast, the music,
and Horton's dances could compensate for the play's weaknesses.

Doris Rudko remembers that Horton staged a particularly
fine courtroom scene in which singers and dancers were an
unobtrusive but vital part of the action. The scene was tightly
knit and dramatically moving. Horton's work in motion pictures
had taught him to make every image count for something. The
dancers liked Horton, who was unpretentious and boyishly
charming. They respected his professionalism and were impressed
by the seeming ease with which he came up with new
movements when something did not work well.

The costumes were the death blow to the production.
Scenes which had looked fine when rehearsed in blue jeans
became ludicrous in delicately shaded cool pastel colors. As one
reviewer put it, the whole thing came off looking like "denatured
Oklahoma!" The producers had reached their stop-loss point and
Shootin' Star never made it to Broadway.

William Katzell's next major attempt at production
made it to Broadway with some distinction. This time Horton

was not involved. The show was the hit musical *Finian's Rainbow.*

     With the out-of-town opening and closing of *Shootin' Star,* Horton found himself at a crossroads, a time for reappraisal. For the first time in many years he had time to reflect on where he had been and where he was going. With no modern dance productions planned and no talented, energetic dancers to keep busy and employed, he could give some consideration to alternatives for his life which might not involve concert dance in Los Angeles.

     He was forty and no longer dancing. Offers of film work had nearly come to a halt. Nineteen forty-six was a time of transition in Hollywood, and soon the exotic films that he had been called upon to do most often would no longer be made. For him perhaps it was just as well. He had recently completed a potboiler, *Tangier,* at Universal and had hated every moment of it. If he chose, he could have pursued a career in a number of phases of design work. Directing was another possibility. The Stubergh's had a standing invitation to him any time he might choose to work in their business.

     But what about all those years of work? There was little to show of any permanence, but what did it matter? He had often been advised to move to New York, where he would not be so isolated from the mainstream of modern dance and where he would not have to rely only on his own resources for everything from training dancers to building audiences. He considered the possibility of working with serious New York dancers who, like Bella, might be willing to become part of an artistic enterprise and stay long enough to build something of value. Still, his home ground was California. In California he had produced everything of quality he had ever done. The outdoors was essential to him, no matter what work he chose to do, for this was where he went for repose and to gather strength. He loved and needed the feel of soil under his feet. New York was a temptation, but only for a while. Oddly refreshed by his few years away from concert work, he was beginning to get new ideas.

He had once built a fine audience in Los Angeles. It was an erratic and elusive audience, true, but at the high point of his earlier career he could attract thousands to the major theaters in the city. He and William Bowne once again discussed the idea of a community theater. They had tried it with some success at the Norma Gould Studio. The minimal cost of theater rental had made frequent performances feasible. More works were tried out, and the dancers had had numerous opportunities to grow through performance. The greatest luxury had been ample time to rehearse on the stage where the work was to be performed. Although he was now deeply involved in his work at the U.C.L.A. Art Department, Bowne was willing to try again with Horton. Their work together had always taken an enormous amount of strength and dedication, but the returns had been stimulating and rewarding. His association with Horton had, in fact, led Bowne to the career which was to be his life's work, teaching art.

The venture was unthinkable without Bella Lewitzky, who had moved to Chicago to be near her husband, Newell Reynolds, who was in the Navy. (They had married in 1940.) Horton wrote her, asking if she was still interested in their old dream project of a theater academy for dance. Lewitzky replied that she was very interested, but with one important reservation. She had always objected to Horton's propensity for using large numbers of people on the stage, many of whom were far from ready for performance. It often fell to her, as assistant choreographer, to make these "extras" as nearly presentable as possible. She answered him:

> Yes. But I am not interested in training fifty people. It is
> too difficult; there are too many of them with two left

feet. I've done this for years, and nothing of excellence comes out on the stage because there are too many dancers and there is too little time. Would this interest you: A small, intimate, excellent company that can get paid—I don't care what, $1.00 a day—just enough that they can afford to work continuously without constant changeover?

Horton agreed, but it was not a promise he was to keep.

dance theater

Once settled in Los Angeles, Horton, William Bowne, Lewitzky, and her husband, Newell Reynolds, who were to be co-directors of the theater, pooled their ideas. The objectives of the theater and school were to be simple and straightforward. The school would be run on the academy principle, with the development of a sequence of learning experiences from childhood to performing maturity. The theater would furnish an environment in which a select group of accomplished dancers could perform often enough to mature not only in individual roles but in the general art of performance. It would provide an opportunity for small guest groups and solo artists to appear in an intimate theater and at a reasonable cost to them. Those who wished to learn about and practice the technical aspects of theater would have numerous opportunities to do so. Good theater dance would be available to the community for a modest admission price—for some three years it was $1.50. The partners would at last have a theater in which to develop their creative work without the crushing financial burden of theater rental.

The following appeared on a 1948 registration flyer for Dance Theater:

A professional attitude in all students is the aim of the school because such an attitude means fuller integration,

115

participation, and acceptance of responsibility. The
standards of the school are aimed toward social integration
and the gaining of technics which embrace more than
step and rhythm dancing. The technics employed include
the use of the complete body—correct posture and body
alignment—skill technics balanced by fantasy development
and improvisation—pantomime and acting—graded dances—
folk dance and derivatives—theater dance—dance arts and
production. The theater is designed to encourage
professional attainment of the highest standards and to
develop artists for the adult company.

But in 1946 all the directors had were a small amount of cash,
four pairs of hands, and a great vision.

After months of searching for a theater site, they came
upon a 4000-square-foot building at 7566 Melrose Avenue in
West Hollywood. The building was a little too narrow and the
rent was high, but the location was excellent. The quonset
construction with its unusually high roof would make the
creation of a stage area relatively simple. A recent fire had gutted
the building, so they could get right to work on redesigning the
interior.

R. M. Schindler, a brilliant architect formerly associated
with Frank Lloyd Wright, acted as advisor to the project and
helped in the face-lifting of the building from a commonplace-
looking pseudo-Spanish storefront to a tasteful rectilinear modern
facade. Schindler also devised a method for constructing the
dance floor on top of two-by-fours, on edge, resting on sections
of war-surplus neoprene air hose. The floor proved to be
amazingly resilient and remained so. Another Schindler idea,
which was to prove more efficient than comfortable, was to vary
the height of the moulded plastic benches which served for
seating, rather than attempt the difficult, cumbersome, and
expensive job of raking the entire house.

The stage area was approximately a thirty-foot square, larger than the auditorium section of the building. There were 133 seats when the theater opened. Fourteen seats were later removed to relieve crowding. Horton had favored the idea of a three-quarter thrust stage, but the size limitations of the building made this impossible. The stage area was masked by a system of louvers which were originally simply painted flats installed at appropriate angles. In 1950 solid panels covered with gypsum board were installed to comply with the fire department regulations. Horizontal louvers were used to mask the ceiling of the proscenium stage.

Mounting overhead lights between the louvers was an extremely difficult job. Vertical pipes were individually suspended from the roof of the building to cover the upstage areas. These could be moved as required with a specially constructed nine-foot platform on dolly wheels. Side lighting was a simpler affair. Pipes mounted between the louvers served to support one to three instruments. Sometimes an instrument was left on the floor for special effects. A conventional vertical stand just inside the proscenium on both sides and an ante-proscenium pipe made more conventional lighting techniques possible. A total of thirty-two instruments were eventually available, but they produced a serious problem. Since the four dimmers could handle only a limited wattage, Horton's special effects often required almost gymnastic manipulations on the part of the lighting crew to effect the complex split-second repluggings required for a cue.

Behind the stage were an L-shaped studio, restrooms, dressing rooms, a sewing room ("home" to Horton for many years), a narrow costume room, and an open-air scene dock equipped with power saws, spray-painting equipment, and a gas stove for glue and dye work. At the front of the theater a ramped entryway was flanked by two small rooms. The one on the right doubled as school office and box office. The left one, originally intended as a class-viewing area, was used as a photo gallery.

The close proximity of the audience to the performers and the general intimacy of the house presented Horton and his dancers with a unique set of problems. The theater illusion was difficult to create with the audience able to see and sometimes be sprinkled by the perspiration of the dancers. The dancers had to learn to modulate their projection to the presence of the audience only a few feet away. Also, greater precision was required, since the slightest flaw in performance could be seen at such close range. Movement on the floor had to be equally precise for at Dance Theater the floor was part of the figure-ground relationship. On the positive side, every nuance of timing and space usage could be calculated weeks in advance of actual performance. More exciting to Horton, however, was the possibility of experimenting in his choreography with areas beyond the stage.

During this period of preparation the Lester Horton Dancers made an appearance in Irwin Parnes' International Folk Dance Festival. Representing American Jazz, the group presented *Barrel House*, with Bella Lewitzky, Herman Boden, Rudi Gernreich, and Carl Ratcliff. Divided into three sections, "Bordello Sob," "Gut Bucket," and "Gully Low," the work, with a New Orleans setting, dealt with the degradation of prostitution. The original score by Anita Metz included jazz piano, the clicking of a horse's jawbone and words shouted by the dancers. (See page 225.) On the same program, Ruth St. Denis performed her timeless *White Jade*.

It took two years of piecemeal building before the theater was opened for performances. Whenever there was a little money left over after the school's expenses were paid, some more building material was purchased. Newell Reynolds was in charge of construction. Something of a perfectionist, he was at the same time adaptable and ingenious at finding inexpensive solutions to building problems. Reynolds had given up performing when he went into the Navy and could now devote his full time and energy to construction work, freeing the others to teach and prepare works for the first Dance Theater season. Most of the other dancers helped when and as they could, but Reynolds did a great deal of the actual construction himself. Between jobs and rehearsals the male dancers would help out with the heavier work while the ladies sewed and painted. As the work neared completion, Horton and Bowne outlined decorative designs and lettering which anyone with a few spare hours could fill in with colors. The exterior of the theater was painted a rich chocolate brown. The large sign across the top of the building was a golden yellow with the words *dance theater,* all in lower case letters, painted in brown.

Herman Boden recalls watching Horton scratching his head, almost until it bled, as he pondered possible alternatives to design or color questions. Connie Finch remembers that he would sometimes stand outside of the unfinished theater in the warm Southern California sunlight, intently watching the expressions on people's faces as they walked by. If a passerby showed any interest, Horton would take time to tell him what was going on and extend an invitation to see the performances. His dazzling smile would animate his impish face whenever he spoke about the theater to friends or strangers. It was a happy time for him—perhaps the happiest in his life. The very air seemed to be filled with the promise of a cherished dream about to come true.

In addition to his construction work, Reynolds was handling business matters for the school, including the voluminous correspondence involved in securing government approval of Dance Theater for study under the G.I. Bill of Rights. His work was successful, and at one time or another within the next few years, nineteen veterans took advantage of the study opportunity, bringing much needed income to the school.

George Allen, Nelson Barclift, Kenneth Bartmess, and Carl
Ratcliff all became company members. Under a cooperative
agreement among the partners, Newell Reynolds' "salary" for his
work during this period (about 16 hours daily) was $20.00 per
week. The others drew similar amounts, and everything else went
back into the theater. Reynolds recalls hammering in time with
the drum-beats of the class behind the studio doors in order not
to lose precious time a few weeks before opening night. The last
seats were installed in the early morning hours of opening day:
May 22, 1948.

For the opening of the theater, Horton designed an
oblong blood-red program cover with handsome free-form
drawings in white. This was to become the Dance Theater logo.
The entire company autographed each copy of the program as a
souvenir for the long-awaited opening.

Contrary to his promise to Lewitzky, Horton used
considerably more than six well-trained dancers in the program,
creating a discord which was to develop to the detriment of
their relationship. Along with the technically proficient dancers
there were those who were not ready for a stage appearance, and
Lewitzky felt that the entire presentation was weakened. But her
irritation was overshadowed by the excitement of the theater's
first season.

Totem Incantation opened the program. It was based on
Coming of Age ceremonies among Northern American Indians.
Carl Ratcliff danced the lead role of the Shaman. Lewitzky
recalled:

> He accompanied himself on a large, stylized hand drum,
> and with voice—guttural calls and sounds. Here again
> Lester used instrument and voice along with movement.
> The sets were two-sided flats with round holes covered
> with string fringe. All entrances were made through these
> holes as though through the round door of a hut. The

> flats were manipulated by two figures in black, so that
> the screens constantly changed shape. The audience saw
> them in motion, but did not see the figures manipulating
> them.

This exercise in nostalgia barely escaped monotony. Though this work was not popular with audiences or the co-directors of the theater, Horton nevertheless watched each performance with deep affection. It seems to have filled a need in him to nod kindly at his beginnings now that he was, in a sense, starting again.

The Beloved was another matter. This piece had been in preparation for almost a year. A fascinating work film, made by Leo Salkin, shows Horton setting the dance on Lewitzky and Brahm van den Berg, two superb performing artists at work with a fine choreographer. For Dance Theater performances the male part was done by Herman Boden, who provided strong and effective support for the demanding role created for Lewitzky. The work was compact; the movements and mood built with inevitability to the chilling dramatic climax. Such a short work with so many remarkable lifts would, in other hands, seem nothing more than a tour de force, but Horton's sensitivity and the flawless execution made the work emerge as something of a wonder. *The Beloved* has been recorded in Labanotation and is presently in the repertory of several dance companies.

The program was rounded out by the third major revision of *Salome*, described in the program notes as "A study in the pathology of decadence." Horton did both the costumes and the accompaniment for this and succeeding versions. Having spent years studying, collecting, and experimenting with percussion instruments, he felt, at last, ready to create a major score by himself. A formidable undertaking, since he never had learned to read music beyond the barest essentials. Aaron Copland later remarked that this version of *Salome* was the best percussion piece for dance he had ever heard. There were those who disagreed about the merits of the score, but it was unquestionably a near-perfect realization of the needs of the work. The accompaniment was played live for the first performances. Dancers and apprentices sat behind a huge scrim at the rear of the stage with the sizable collection of instruments, furiously concentrating on the difficult score. The human voice was interwoven with the myriad sounds. Fascinating shifts in rhythm and rising crescendos combined to achieve an almost symphonic effect. Horton again utilized variously shaped platforms and ramps for *Salome.*

In an apologia written two years later Horton said:

> [Earlier versions] . . . were to a considerable extent
> dependent on the Wildean concept. Which is to say, a
> relatively superficial one from the standpoint of inner
> motivations, for Wilde was fascinated by the surface
> terror, the superficial shock, the poetry of words and
> images . . . This time I started to examine the motives
> more thoroughly. Wilde had receded . . . I turned, I
> think, to Freud.

Although Frank Eng was the "ghost writer" for this apologia, there is little reason to doubt that the choreographer was thinking along these lines. In the work, however, there is decidedly little to bear out any in-depth psychological exploration of the protagonist. Horton may have seen as Freudian his development of the character of Herodias, who very pointedly goads Salome on rather than trying to discourage her in any way. The range of Salome's perversity, too, was broadened in this version as hints of onanism, foot fetishism, and incest appeared (to be developed in later versions), but the work remained essentially a powerful theatrical statement and not one that is psychologically revealing to any great extent. Horton had, in common with Wilde, a desire to challenge the outer limits of his audiences' moral sensibilities and like Wilde he was at his best dazzling his audience rather than dealing with complex subtleties.

The role of Salome in Horton's choreodrama is among the most challenging ever created in the modern dance repertory and requires an actress-dancer of considerable skill and endurance. Depending on the version, the character is on stage for 32 to 37 minutes and is almost continually in motion. Horton's choreography was *never* easy to perform.

Performances in numerous versions of the work gave Lewitzky great assurance and understanding in her interpretation of the role. In this mature rendering she was a sensuous and forceful wanton who moved the piece to frightening heights of tension.

Powerful interpretations of their roles by Herman Boden as Herod, Frances Spector as Herodias, Erik Johns as John the Baptist, and a brilliant reading of the part of the Eunuch by Rudi Gernreich brought the audience to its feet applauding, screaming and stamping for numerous curtain calls from the company. Dance Theater was at last a reality!

It was more than an exciting opening night that was being cheered by that first audience. Many were there who, years before, had gone to Norma Gould's studio to see workshop performances by a promising young choreographer and his group. They were cheering the fulfillment of that early promise. Lester Horton and his hard-working associates had created a place where dancers and choreographers could see the concrete results of hard work and dedication. A theater had been built— the first permanent repertory dance theater on the West Coast, and a distinctive technique was being taught, a technique which would train and develop many skilled artists. Los Angeles in the early 1950s was still a cultural wasteland and yet in that least likely of all places and times, in a milieu notably lacking in com-

mitment and vision, they had risen above intramural jealousies
and the lethargy of a community to pursue an ideal.

Although the Los Angeles press was, for the most part,
highly favorable in reviews of the opening season of Dance
Theater, an unpleasant note was struck by the music critic of
the *Los Angeles Times,* Albert Goldberg. Mr. Goldberg was
reviewing dance for the most influential paper in the city, but he
apparently had not taken the trouble to look into recent
developments in the art form and chose to conceal his lack of
erudition with superciliousness. He wrote:

> There is a good deal of interest to be discovered in the
> activities of this courageous band of enthusiasts as well as
> at least one example of outstanding talent. Mr. Horton is
> the choreographer and the style in general is that of the
> advanced left. The dancing is all of the barefoot variety,
> which, if you sit close, as you cannot help doing, does
> not leave you with too much respect for the pedal
> extremities of the human body as objects of beauty.

At the time, dancing "of the barefoot variety" had been
a recognized art form for nearly fifty years, dating from Isadora
Duncan's early concert appearances in Europe. Nowhere in the
review is there any mention of the uniqueness of Dance Theater
in the American dance world or recognition of the fact that
some of the members of the "courageous band of enthusiasts"
had been at work in Los Angeles for twenty years. To all intents
and purposes as far as most of the major Los Angeles newspapers
were concerned, after only a five-year absence from the scene,
Horton was being treated as a newcomer. With a few exceptions,
he had received more knowledgeable criticism than this in the
1930s, when modern dance was still in its adolescent years.

Unaccountably, Horton's program notes during his five
years of Dance Theater activity go steadily from bad to worse.

They are often misleading and, through the years, they become increasingly wordy and pretentious. *The Beloved* is introduced by these words on the program, "Out of an era of dogma and women's servility comes a theme of fanatic bigotry leading to violence." Horton had found his inspiration for *The Beloved* in a newspaper article about a man in the Midwest who had beaten his wife to death with a Bible because of some suspected infidelity. The dance tells the story very well; the program notes add nothing and are actually a bit cumbersome. Mr. Goldberg wrote in the same review with some justification:

> Never handy at discovering ulterior meanings in such
> things, we missed the dogma, the servility and bigotry,
> but there was certainly a good deal of violence,
> culminating in a harrowing neck swinging sequence and
> realistic throttling.

He must have seen a bit more than neck swinging and throttling, for in the article he compared Lewitzky's performance to that of the superb dramatic ballerina Nora Kaye, who was at the time her idol and, later, her daughter's namesake.

An entirely different reaction came from Frank Eng, who had come to Dance Theater as a reviewer for the *Los Angeles Daily News.* He was overwhelmed by the production and especially by the performance of the leading dancer. He wrote, "The inescapable and towering impression is the indelible one left by the astounding work of . . . Bella Lewitzky. . . . We have never witnessed a more electrifying piece of work than her title role in *The Beloved.*" And prophetically, "Out of such a group should come our future dancing finds, our choreographers and an influence on drama and the arts in general that cannot fail to be of import to artists throughout the land." In a 1954 interview Eng remembered some of his first impressions of Dance Theater:

It was with no small appreciation that I found that with
Lester Horton, at his Dance Theater and School, individual
human dignity was held at the inviolate level. Children of
three were treated as individuals with their own rights and
sensibilities—not to be talked down to. And race and
creed were but interesting differentiations of individuals
who were always different from one another anyway.

After numerous subsequent visits to the theater he offered his
services as press agent, gratis, out of a deep admiration for the
gifted young artists and their mentor. Within a year he and
Horton were sharing an apartment. It was a friendship which was
to change the course of Eng's life, for when Horton died
he inherited the guardianship of Dance Theater.

One of his first ideas as press agent in 1949 was to
publicize the coming season as "Choreo '50." Successive seasons
would be identified in the same way. Soon after undertaking the
work, Eng began to encourage Horton to develop the lighter side
of the repertory to help bolster attendance at the theater. It was
advice which ran exactly counter to the wishes of his co-directors,
but Horton, tempted to do some work in a lighter vein, went
ahead with the advice, ignoring the real possibility that he might
be causing friction with his colleagues.

Somehow anticipating the sexual revolution of the 1960s
Horton was moving further into a stylistic range which was
frankly sensual; he was ready for a period of *play* with these
new materials. He felt, moreover, that he could continue to work
on serious dances at the same time, with no loss of quality. He
had convinced himself that he could, indeed, do "something to
please everybody." The results would be seen in the next two
seasons of Dance Theater offerings.

By the opening of the 1949 season, William Bowne had
quietly left Dance Theater to marry Portia Woodbury of the

Dance Theater. (Photo by Ernest Reshovsky.)

original Horton group and to concentrate on developing his
career as an artist and art teacher. He would return to Dance
Theater briefly to teach and design, but only as a guest. Horton
told his closest friends that he was very happy for Bill and
Portia, but a few perceptive ones realized that an irreplaceable
balancing force had left the theater and Horton's life. To cover
the gap left by Bowne's departure, an elaborate company Plan of
Organization was drawn up. In it dozens of tasks involved in the
theater's activities were described, establishing specific duties and
chains of command. Newell Reynolds, who was working on a
degree in architecture at the same time, was Dance Theater
Production Manager and responsible for seeing to it that the Plan
of Organization worked.

      Principal dancers for the season were Carl Ratcliff, Louisa
Kreck, Kenneth Bartmess, Connie Finch, Rudi Gernreich, Marge
Berman, Nelson Barclift, and the thirteen-year-old prodigy,
Sondra Orans. Alvin Ailey and Don Martin were on the stage
crew and a young, gawky girl, Carmen de Lavallade, was
experiencing her first performances in workshops and lecture-
demonstrations. She was only seventeen. That same year her
cousin, Janet Collins, who had also studied with Horton, was to
have a memorable debut at the 92nd Street "Y" in New York
City, and a few years later she was to become the first black
Première Danseuse of the Metropolitan Opera Company. Her trip
east was partially financed through weekend solo performances
at Dance Theater. One day de Lavallade too would grace the
stage of the "Met."

      For the 1949 season the directors of Dance Theater
decided to try out the repertory concept by playing completely
different programs on alternate weekend nights. It made sense to
capitalize on the huge success of the previous season by offering
Totem Incantation, Salome, and *Beloved* on Friday nights. The
Saturday evening program of new works included *A Touch of
Klee and Delightful 2,* inspired by the paintings of Paul Klee

Salome, 1948; Bella Lewitzky. (Photo by Leo Salkin.)

The Park, 1949;
Bella Lewitzky,
Carl Ratcliff.
(Photo by Constantine.)

Totem Incantation, 1948;
Rudi Gernreich,
Carl Ratcliff,
Erik Johns.
(Photo by Constantine.)

Soldadera, 1950; Bella Lewitzky.
One of this set appeared on the cover of *Dance Magazine*.
(Photo by Constantine.)

Warsaw Ghetto, 1949; Bella Lewitzky.
(Photo by Constantine.)

and utilizing a complex arrangement of swings as part of the
setting; *Barrel House*—completely reworked from the earlier
version; *Bench of the Lamb, Warsaw Ghetto,* and *The Park.*

Perhaps of the greatest interest, though least successful in
the program, was the topical work, *The Park.* Horton set out to
tell a story of police brutality toward Mexican-Americans in Los
Angeles. Basing his scenario on a true incident reported in the
Los Angeles papers, he attempted a modern treatment of the
William Butler Yeats' play-for-dancers idea. The spoken word
was used extensively with recorded sounds of city life in the
background. The movement was a combination of dance and
natural, untheatricalized motion. The dancers had made several
trips to a park in a Mexican neighborhood in order to study the
rhythm and gestures of the people. Shoes were worn in the
piece, and Louisa Kreck, who had to learn to maneuver about in
high heels for the first time in her life, provided great cause for
amusement during rehearsals. The settings by Bowne were
stylized with an element of fantasy. *The Park* was frankly
experimental and, from all accounts, neither effective theater nor
good dance, but a bold attempt to explore new possibilities,
risking failure at a time when neither Horton nor Dance Theater
could well afford it. In place of the familiar choreographic
credit on the program were the words, "Directed by Lester
Horton."

Barrel House must have affected Alvin Ailey, who later
would use a similar theme for his *Roots of the Blues.* The
program notes read: "A series of dances based upon the protests
and miseries suggested in the early forms of music originating in
the parlors and barrel houses of New Orleans." *Bench of the
Lamb* could have been inspired by the rape scene in *Dark of the
Moon.* The innocent girl of the play is transformed in the
Horton scenario, into a lady of doubtful reputation, alternately
played by Connie Finch and Louisa Kreck. To prepare for the
role, Horton sent the young dancers to study skid row whores

and to attend a Holy Roller church. Finch, who had been raised
"very properly," later said, "If you came to Dance Theater with
prejudices and preconceptions you didn't keep them long. Lester
felt that it got in the way of your growth and of course he was
right. He taught all of us how to work."

    Warsaw Ghetto, with a stunning set by artist Keith Finch,
was the third dance on the program to involve social
commentary or protest. A staunch supporter from the old days,
W.E. Oliver of the *Los Angeles Herald and Express* (one of the
few critics that Horton respected), was ecstatic over this
particular piece. He lauded the integration of drama, music, and
scenery and compared its impact with that he had first
experienced on seeing Fokine's *Petrouchka.* Other reactions were
mixed. A few displeased critics faulted the program not for its
heavy topical content but for what seemed to them to be a
fixation on sexuality in the movement vocabulary. This trend in
the work had seriously troubled Horton's co-directors as well.
Years later, Bill Bowne was to say:

> When his work became blatantly erotic I thought it was a
> disintegration. It had always been an important ingredient
> in his material, but Bella and I withdrew every kind of
> approval. Now when I see what the sexual liberation thing
> is like, I realize he was doing what he always did,
> anticipating what was about to happen. To us it seemed
> like he had a tremendous social statement he had to make
> and instead he was doing those things. Of course, now we
> see that it *was* a social statement and it has had a
> sweeping effect on the whole country—the whole world.

    The phrase "withdrew every kind of approval" suggests
the complexity of Horton's demands on his close collaborators.
At the same time that he needed their advice, their talents, and
their discipline, he also needed to be free to make his own final

decisions. They had understood this and had often relented out of their love for him and respect for his creativity. On the other hand, because he vacillated between periods of supreme confidence and wracking insecurity, he needed their approval and unqualified support, even if they strongly disagreed with him. With Bowne's departure that support so essential to his well-being was considerably diminished. Soon it would all be gone.

Early in the season there had been rumblings of discord among the directors. Lewitzky was once again upset by the large number of inexperienced dancers in the program. Also, at the same time that she was disturbed by the content of some of the works, she was wondering whether her contribution to the creative process was being undervalued in the eyes of the public. She asked for, and was given, much deserved choreographic credit on the program. Another source of irritation was Horton's carelessness with accounts. It was simply not within his nature to keep track of monies in a businesslike way.

The season had been mediocre and certainly not up to the expectations set by the previous one. Countless discussions seemed to lead nowhere. A pall began to hang over the theater and, though Horton continued to choreograph prolifically, there were inevitable signs that the quality of work was being affected by the growing tensions.

Modern dance on both coasts seemed to be at a low ebb creatively at this time. Films, too, which so often reflect the health of the arts in this country, were notably poor, as the movie industry attempted to boost sagging box office receipts by announcing, "Movies Are Better Than Ever." As if to prove the fallacy of the statement, Universal Studios made *Bagdad* with Yvonne de Carlo. Horton was Dance Director. It was his sixteenth Hollywood film.

The work which was supposed to be the high point of "Choreo '50," *A Bouquet for Molly*, was a fiasco from the beginning. What had started out as a lusty conflict between a Mexican and

a Caucasian for the favors of a frontier gal of high spirits and
low morals was unaccountably watered down by Horton to
include another female character as well as the tap dancing
talents of George Allen. With the conflict practically nonexistent
and poor casting (Sandra Orans was half Bella Lewitzky's age)
the work seemed pallid. It fared no better when performed
by Louisa Kreck, who alternated with Lewitzky in the title role.
The situation was not helped by a disappointing score, especially
commissioned from folk singer Earl Robinson, which had
been expensive by the standards of Dance Theater's tiny
budget. It had the familiar slick sound of a motion picture
score. *Bouquet for Molly* was below par for Dance Theater
and should have been removed from the repertory and reworked.
But the score would have had to be discarded and there was
no money for another. Moreover, the season had opened, and
Horton was physically exhausted and emotionally drained
by events in his personal life and the tensions of
the theater.

"Danzón," to Aaron Copland's *Danzón Cubano,* a duet
for Lewitzky and Carl Ratcliff, made matters worse. It was
precisely the kind of sexy ethnic fun dance that Horton enjoyed
putting together and she hated to perform. "Danzón" was part
of a four-dance suite, *Estilo de Tú,* a catch-all format
reminiscent of *Something to Please Everybody* from a decade
earlier. "Frevo" was an authentically-based Brazilian festival
dance; "Soldadera," a well-crafted but passionless solo for Bella
Lewitzky in which a female soldier mourns the death of her
soldier husband; and "Xango," a fetishistic invocation to the god
of lightning, a tour de force for Louisa Kreck. Each of these was
drastically reworked for later seasons, but in "Choreo '50" only
"Xango" had a glimmer of Horton's theatrical brilliance. In his
efforts to please everybody, he had pleased nobody, least of all
himself.

El Robozo (The Shawl) was the major work on the
program. It was a greatly improved reworking of the previous

season's *The Park* but still a curiously unmoving work, considering the theme. Horton had simply lost his feeling for dance as propaganda and *El Robozo* showed it. As in the previous season, the most interesting aspects of the piece were in the innovative uses of décor, sound score, and costume.

Horton found himself more pained and irritated than pleased with the favorable reviews of "Choreo '50." He and everyone else at Dance Theater knew that the program was not a good one, and yet several writers had praised the evening highly. Only a few of the reviewers at this time seemed to understand what Horton was trying to accomplish with the theater and what its great potential was. The others, who were in the majority, mistakenly believed that the goal of the presentations was purely entertainment. They tended to confuse flashiness and surface polish with artistry and imagination and seemed to be almost blindly supportive. Horton had never needed or wanted this kind of support.

He must have been thinking of this season's reviews when he said in his lecture-demonstration a year later, "We are fortunate when we can find a critic who can discern the able from the spurious." And he may have been remembering the conflicting opinions of Miriam Geiger and Darr Smith about Carl Ratcliff's performance when he said on the same occasion, "The contradictions [of the critics] sum up something quite beyond our imagination." Darr Smith had written in the *Daily News,* "Running close to her [Bella Lewitzky] was Carl Ratcliff, a young man of superb physique, haunting face and superlative execution." In the only completely negative review, Miriam Geiger had said, "In 'Frevo' the enthusiasm came through in spite of the far from good dancing of Mr. Carl Ratcliff, who was bad not only in this but in 'Danzón' and 'A Bouquet for Molly.' "

Geiger, writing in the *Los Angeles Tribune,* had understood that something was wrong at Dance Theater. She began her review by telling us point blank that she did not like the concept of the choreodrama, "These [choreodramas] invariably sacrifice dancing to the story they attempt to tell. And because the story is frequently elemental, it rarely succeeds in holding the attention."

Then followed the part which must have rocked Dance Theater a few times:

> And what happened to Bella Lewitzky? I felt myself waiting through "Soldadera," "Danzon" and "El Robozo" for one spark which would have mirrored the Lewitzky of *The Beloved,* that exquisite fragment which she does so superbly — but it never came. She was never anywhere near it. No one can fool me about Lewitzky. She can dance now, as she has always been able to dance. Then why did she not — why did her dancing just skirt dancing and never touch it? Is it because (as I suspect) the program and the choreography were produced carelessly? This is not merely because Miss Lewitzky did not extend on Saturday night, but because it seemed the entire cast did not FEEL anything they were dancing, not even the propaganda.

Near the end of the article she wrote:

> So, Miss Lewitzky and Mr. Horton, let's get back to *The Beloved* . . . and *Bench of the Lamb* and last, but not at all least, *A Touch of Klee and Delightful 2.* That was real Dance Theater and we loved it.

But, of course, it was too late. A few weeks after the opening of "Choreo '50" Bella and Newell Reynolds informed Horton that they wished to dissolve the Dance Theater partnership and requested a formal meeting to effect the dissolution. The tension had been building for some time, and the quality and content of the new season had led to the final decision. Horton was plainly tired of concentrating on works of social significance and was less malleable and willing to negotiate than he had been. Lewitzky had come to dislike performing in the commercial work, and the blatant sensuality of his new lighter pieces troubled her. She understood how Horton was challenged by the skills required by motion picture work—fascinated by the possibilities of the camera, but she felt that film work drained vitality from the activities of the theater. Another problem was developing over differences in teaching methods. Horton's teaching was, more than ever, intuitive, inspired, and exploring. Miss Lewitzky, he felt, was becoming too precise, careful, and balletic. He wished to train artists; it seemed to him that she was interested only in building technicians. Characteristically, he did not speak of this; but the tension was there.

Most of the responsibility of leadership for the company fell to him, and it was not within his nature to take a firm hand when serious problems arose. He depended on a precarious balance between the creative and personal needs of everyone importantly involved in Dance Theater. When the delicate balance had been upset before, Bill Bowne had always been there to mend the situation.

One can almost follow the growth of another aspect of the problem between the directors and the attempts at solution by comparing program credits in successive seasons. In 1948, credits are listed haphazardly. No name is featured above others; the star of the event is the joint accomplishment, "Dance Theater." By 1950, under the banner, Dance Theater Company are the words Managing Director and the name Newell Reynolds in the only bold-face type. Both Horton's and Lewitzky's names are in lighter print with the rest of the company, although each is given joint choreographic credit under the individual pieces. For fifteen years the venture had been known primarily by Horton's name, and attempts to balance the attention given by the public and press were not very successful. It is a familiar problem in small-scale artistic enterprises. As the younger artists mature they need increased recognition and eventually have to go where they are not in the shadow of another artist's creativity.

During the painful meeting held on February 15, 1950, at which the terms of the dissolution of the partnership were discussed, Horton barely spoke. His world was crumbling around him. For years he had been nurtured by the mutual affection and support he had shared with Bill and Bella. Bill Bowne had gone only a year before, and that had been very difficult. Largely on the strength of Bella's and Bill's love for him and belief in him, he had spared nothing of himself for that theater. He tried to understand that they had outgrown the need to develop in the artistic climate which his work provided, that they were ready for their own enterprises. At the meeting Lewitzky spoke of the need for creative *lebensraum*.

When would the time have been right for her to leave? Would her debt to him ever be paid, or for that matter his to her? She had been part of his growth as an artist and teacher. He had been deeply dependent on her at the same time that she was developing her art under his inspired teaching. The marvel of the relationship was that it had survived as long as it did. This was partly due to Horton's unique ability to work with co-artists without crowding them out and partly to Lewitzky's passionate dedication and recognition of the rare quality of her teacher. She had been called "Horton's Miracle." Perhaps now the time had come for her to be her own miracle.

When Bella and Newell Reynolds realized that for them the time had passed when they should have left Dance Theater, the belatedness of the decision intensified the urgency of their departure. As in a serious family quarrel old wounds were reopened and unresolved grievances were magnified. The whole affair had the quality of a divorce action in which one or both parties intensify the anger in order to help justify the severity of their actions to themselves.

The dissolution of partnership shook Dance Theater to its foundations. Sides had been taken by company members and the toll was considerable. Carl Ratcliff and Jeri Faubion left with Bella to form a new school, Dance Associates. Lew Brown, who had designed both sets and costumes, and Marge Berman, who danced and taught classes, left also. In order to get started on their own, the Reynoldses needed capital. What they received as a financial settlement was pitiably small in terms of what they had put into Dance Theater. Horton, on the other hand, was left with a theater and an empty bank account. Bella Lewitzky also received the rights to perform *The Beloved,* "Danzon," and "Soldadera," all of which she had helped to create. It somehow seems ironic that the June, 1950 cover of *Dance Magazine* features a beautiful full-length photo by Constantine of Lewitzky in a turning sequence from "Soldadera."

Perhaps as Horton sat listening to the Reynoldses' grievances and terms, he was already planning a partial remedy for the shock. Who would replace Bella? What could he do to restore himself and go on? Angry at himself, angry at Bella and Newell, he entered into a frenzy of creativity that dazzled even those who took his prodigious talents for granted.

Within a few days of the dissolution meeting Horton announced that he was going to do a mid-season revival of *Salome.* Louisa Kreck, a beautiful, willowy dancer who had been with the theater since its opening was the predictable choice to take over the roles created for Lewitzky. She had in fact previously alternated performances of several of those roles and had received excellent notices. She had done equally well with parts created especially for her, such as the lead in "Xango." But Horton had been looking at another young dancer and with an unfailing instinct had seen in lovely Carmen de Lavallade a potential for brilliance. He was not disappointed in his choice. De Lavallade was to develop into one of the finest and most versatile dancers of her time. She remembers his quiet reply when, as a somewhat baffled and excited young woman still in her late teens, she had asked Horton when she could arrange to meet with Bella to start learning the role of Salome, "You are not Bella and she is not you. We will start again." He proceeded to rechoreograph large sections of the piece, making skillful use of the special qualities she was able to bring to it: her lyricism, her feeling for drama, and her youth. Salome, after all, was only a youngster.

Some adjustments were made to conceal her technical shortcomings, and what emerged was a unique combination of youthful freshness with seasoned professionalism. Once again, Horton was developing a highly gifted young artist who would one day rise to the top of her profession. The process was very different from the one he had evolved with Lewitzky, who had been energetic, precise, and challenging. De Lavallade, less of a technician than Lewitzky, was receptive, pliant, and a natural actress. Like Lewitzky, she had drive and a capacity for hard work. Within two years she required no choreographic adjustments to meet Horton's needs, and though scarcely out of her teens she had become an important artist in her profession. Recently, she spoke of Horton's training and later influence on her work:

> Lester taught me how to work from the inside out with imagery. Now if I have something to do, I'll find a way to do it even if it is something very difficult technically. It becomes possible because the right image will strengthen the technique. If I'm not given a reason, I'll find one for myself and if I can't, something is really wrong.

In 1967, Carmen de Lavallade received a *Dance Magazine* award. The citation read, "To Carmen de Lavallade: 'Beauteous

symbol of today's total dancer, she conveys the sensuous
pleasure of movement with simplicity, elegance and superb
control.'" In her acceptance speech de Lavallade told her
audience:

> Long ago, Lester Horton told me that in years to come
> dancers would have to encompass all the areas of the
> theatre . . . And I think he was right. At that time he
> sent me to teachers like Carmelita Maracci, a great ballet
> teacher and great woman. He sent me to study singing,
> to acting classes. I would like to tell young people that
> this was good advice.

In previous years when Horton worked under pressure,
he had impressed his co-workers with his calmness and
concentration. They describe a kind of tranquility about him in
those days, difficult to describe yet deeply felt, when he was
absorbed in a task. Now, with the pain and depression caused by
Lewitzky's departure and the dozens of vexations involved in
launching a new season, Horton seemed to be working purely on
nervous energy. He became fidgety and was constantly in motion
even when he was not at work on the formidable job he had
undertaken.

For the revival of *Salome* he reworked twenty-five
minutes of choreography, taught several highly demanding roles,
designed and constructed new costumes and props, and
re-created and taught the complex percussion score.

There is a strength and exuberance in the costume
sketches Horton drew for the new *Salome* that helps us to
understand the urgency with which he was working; he was
trying to re-create a new Dance Theater out of the wreckage of
the old. The loss of his ideal co-worker had been a severe blow
to his ego. The implications of her angry departure and the

grimness of the separation proceedings haunted him. He seemed to be trying to prove to himself that he was not crippled artistically by her departure. In the next few years he would, in fact, come into his finest and most original period of creativity.

Before the opening of the *Salome* revival on April 7, two more excellent dancers departed the ranks of Dance Theater. Connie Finch decided she needed to spend more time with her growing family and to develop her work as a painter. Both she and her husband Keith had blossomed in their art work during their Dance Theater years. Rudi Gernreich, now internationally known in the fashion world for his innovative ideas, left also to pursue his career as a designer of women's apparel. Both Gernreich, who later helped revolutionize women's fashions with his topless and bra-less designs, and Finch frequently acknowledge a deep debt to Horton for freedom in approaching their work.

A few months later Horton added two more works to the mid-season revival of *Salome*, but the new program gave only a hint of the fruitful period to come. The delightful *Rhythm Section* featured a favorite device: the dancers accompanied themselves in each of the three parts. "Drum Dance" was revived from the early 1940s, "Tinnikaling" was his version of the Philippine dance performed with bamboo poles, and "Stick Dance" utilized small rhythm sticks. *Brown County, Indiana* (See page 228), which told the story of a run-away slave girl who was protected from her pursuer by a Quaker widow and her daughter, was a vehicle for Carmen de Lavallade. The costumes by Rudi Gernreich and sets by William Bowne were handsome and functional, but though the piece had lovely moments it shared a similar fate to that of *The Park*, and for similar reasons: its characters were stereotypes and its message was too obvious.

Since the opening of Dance Theater, Horton had neglected his health even more than he had done in the past. If he had any idea of the seriousness of his heart disorder, he didn't let anyone know it. He tended to overeat for energy, seldom took time off to relax once his day was started, and planned his busy production schedule carelessly, so that the bulk of his work often had to be done at the last minute. Immediately before an opening he sometimes worked two days without sleep and then collapsed from fatigue. Unable to find the time to escape from the pressures of the theater, he would catnap where and when he could, only to be awakened for a class or rehearsal or other urgent business.

In early July, 1950, Lester Horton had his first serious heart attack.

 rebuilding

Frank Eng remembers that on the day Horton was well enough to return to Dance Theater, he approached the doors and hesitated for just a moment, his sagging shoulders and painworn face saying what no words could communicate. He had nearly died meeting the requirements of that theater. Four people were to have shared the work that now had become his sole responsibility, with only Frank to help. But, if he paused to consider other options, it was only briefly. The sum total of his life's work was behind those red doors. He entered the building.

His doctors had asked him to return to work slowly, to follow a careful diet, and to take rest periods. One suggested that he drink a bit of wine to relax his nerves. That was the only advice about his health that he followed, and for the first time in his life he started to drink regularly. At first his drinking had a kind of balance to it and was only a trifle more than moderate. As the thought of death became increasingly frightening to him he perversely became more neglectful of himself, with little thought or care for what he needed to do to survive. He put on weight and continued to work long hours without rest. Later, when his drinking became heavier, he refused to recognize the possible consequences. If anything, he seemed to be doing the opposite of what would be beneficial to him. When this was brought to his attention, he rationalized that the drinking helped him in his work. Work, he told friends, would refresh and renew him. His plan for self-renewal involved preparing a new season and the complete reworking of his training techniques.

He and Eng moved into the sewing room of the studio. His illness had completely drained him financially, and saving the cost of an apartment would help to make the next season possible. Yet, the studio was no place for a man who needed to balance his work schedule with rest and relaxation. Often, after only four or five hours of sleep, the phone would ring and Horton's day would begin—a day in which he was teaching, choreographing, and designing as well as helping Eng in the administration of the school and theater. He should have been sleeping twice that many hours.

"Choreo '51" was projected as a series of "Fun Dances," and for the first time in years Horton was working without any pressure from his colleagues to devote substantial amounts of his energy to social statement. These "Fun Dances," colorful explorations of movement, textures, shapes, and sounds, were an important impetus to his artistic renewal. They gave him an opportunity to indulge his rich sense of theatrical fantasy and opened new channels of fresh creativity. Frank Eng seemed to understand this aspect of his friend's artistic needs and encouraged him to work as he wished. A few notes on the "Choreo '51" programs indicate Horton's thinking at the time.

> Choreo '51 marks a return for Dance Theater to Lester Horton's original concept of the fusion of theater elements with dance, returning the choreographer to fields he helped pioneer in afro-carib [sic], ethnic material . . . it re-establishes him firmly as an artist of varied expression . . . [and elsewhere] . . . dances that reaffirm the freedom, the beauty and sheer kinesthetic joy of the art . . . Modern dance that owes no allegiance but to the art of bodily movement.

Another, more practical factor involved in the development of this repertory was, once again, an attempt to create pieces which would lead to paying work for the dancers. After the sour experiences of the past several years, Horton decided to ask his principal performers to sign contracts assuring that in exchange for their training—none of them paid for classes—they would be available for concert and commercial work for a period of at least one year. (See page 240.) Too many dancers in the past several years had worked with him just long enough to qualify as professionals and then had taken the first lucrative job offer that came along. It was not a choice he enjoyed making, but he had been stunned to realize that none of the nine dancers of the earlier 1950 season was still at Dance Theater, and only Carmen de Lavallade and Jack Dodds, who were featured in the midseason program, remained. He had to start once again nearly from scratch to build a new performing ensemble. One of the new company members, Vida Solomon, was still a teenager. Within a year she was joined by two gifted products of the children's school, Lelia Goldoni and Misaye Kawasumi, both also in their mid-teens, and Joyce Trisler, only a year older. Some others like Eleanor Johnson, an ex-Katherine Dunham dancer, and James Truitte, who had performed in several musicals, were attracted to Dance Theater by its opportunities for excellent training and frequent performances. Truitte was later to become a mainstay at Dance Theater and an outstanding teacher of Horton's techniques.

Initially, activities were organized around the concept of both a concert group and a commercial unit, in an effort to keep somewhat separate identities. After a few months, however, the Lester Horton Dancers (commercial) and the Dance Theater Company (concert) comprised the same dancers. The dancers were paid union wages for any commercial work which could be found for them. Often, as in the past, Horton accepted no compensation either for his choreography or for the brilliant

costumes which were always costly and time-consuming to
create. Most of the fee for any night club or TV work was
equally divided among the dancers.

"Choreo '51" opened with *Tropic Trio.* The first dance
was "Batucada," a Brazilian work dance. It was followed by
"Cumbia," a Panamanian-inspired erotic duet in which the male
manipulates a glowing candle as both dancers' bodies undulate
sensuously. The completely revised "Frevo" often startled the
audience when the dancers, swinging and twirling umbrellas,
burst through the doors at the rear of the theater in an
explosion of color and sound. Based on street dances of Rio de
Janeiro at Carnival time, the piece was deceptively simple, if
wild in appearance. In reality it was an endurance test for even
the hardiest dancers to perform well. The company thrived on
such challenging works, and its members' technical abilities
increased rapidly as a result. Among the dancers left gasping for
breath at the end of "Frevo" was a U.C.L.A. Romance Language
student, Alvin Ailey.

The outstanding dance of the trio was "Cumbia," with
Carmen de Lavallade's lovely light-brown skin shimmering against
a full, white, ruffled costume as she danced with handsome,
Slavic-looking Jack Dodds. A sexy interracial love duet was quite
daring in 1951, but it scarcely raised a brow at Dance Theater,
where people had come to expect to see such things. The
trouble was to come later when Las Vegas agents refused to
book the interracial company. "Cumbia" received praise both as
a concert piece and as night club material. It was to serve both
purposes well for the next few years and in addition it was
featured, in different versions, in two of Horton's films. The
Brazilian Ambassador had been invited to the opening of
"Choreo '51" and delighted Horton by praising the authenticity
of the colorful pieces and by asking him when he had been in
South America.

The other flashy work on the program, the technically
demanding suite *On the Upbeat,* was divided into four parts:
"Brushoff Blues," styled after the flamenco *cante hondo;*

"Kathak," in the North Indian dance style; a take-off on
Burmese dance, "Pwe Bop"; and "Chassidic," an exuberant
Jewish feast dance, which somehow fitted nicely into the group.
James Truitte remembered:

> When the curtain opened on "Kathak" you saw pink,
> yellow, orange, green, blue, purple, red, silver. With a
> special lavender light on the fabrics we had tie-dyed, it
> looked like flames. Before we moved, the audience was
> applauding.

Critics found the suite "breathtakingly colorful," "spirited,"
and "spontaneous." Horton felt they were among his best lighter
pieces.

Since the late 1930s his designs had boldly enhanced the
sexual attractiveness of the dancers, baffling those who associated
modern dance with long jersey dresses or a cross between winter
underwear and a shroud. The women were often barelegged or
dressed in sensuously flowing full skirts. Bodices were fitted and
often strapless. The men wore open-necked shirts or were bare-
chested; trousers were tightly fitted. Both sexes were made to
look alluring and confident in their sexuality. In tone, if not in
actual appearance, it was a 1970s look.

The reactions of professionals in the field to the two
groups of "Fun Dances" were mixed. Commercially oriented
choreographers were obviously impressed, and a few indulged in
that sincerest form of flattery, imitation. Horton was astonished
to see a near replica of one of his dances on national television
within weeks after the well-known choreographer of the show
had visited Dance Theater. To some in the Los Angeles area,
however, who saw modern dance as a strictly high-minded
endeavor, the new pieces seemed garish and cheap. The sensuous
physicality of the ethnically inspired works appeared to them to
be out of place on the concert stage and the verdict was that
they were *not* serious art. Horton had heard that before when he

had done *Something to Please Everybody* in the late 1930s. Now he felt he had earned the right to work as he wished to in his own theater and that these pieces were as essential a part of his expression as his most serious works had been. He often quoted Martha Graham's famous dictum, "There are only two kinds of dance, good and bad."

In this mood of reaffirmation he created one of his finest works, *Another Touch of Klee.* For this reworking of the 1949 Klee offering he obtained the permission of Stan Kenton to use several of the progressive jazz musician's short works: "Mirage," "Trajectories," "Incident in Jazz," and "Theme for Sunday." The new piece was made up of four choreographic excursions which alternated between moods of lyricism, satire, and whimsy in a haunting atmosphere enhanced by subtle, dreamlike lighting.

"Landscape of Longing" opens with a solo figure turning elegantly on *pointe in plié.* She is wearing only one toe shoe and a mask is held in front of her face. Her hand is on a blue rope which mysteriously divides the stage space. When another figure joins her, she lets her mask fall and exits, and at the same moment a male dancer drops from above to join the second girl in a dreamlike duet. The opening figure re-enters, crosses the stage with another rope, and the dream-lovers are separated. The stage is now set for "Dilemma." The first young lady reappears now wearing two toe shoes and a harlequin mask and holding an ingenious "devil trap," a prop which Horton had created using sticks, string, and ping-pong balls. She observes two robot-like men intent on following the pattern of the ropes. Low key lighting on the rope setting gives the stage a heightened three-dimensional effect. (The program note read, " 'Dilemma' caricatures the cheerful idea that people are puppets manipulated by a devilish fate.") Once again, the restless one must change things; she removes the ropes. In "Dance of the Red Skirts" the two male dancers, now her accomplices, hand her three sets of matching red skirts, hats, and nosegays which she fussily hangs on the

reinstated ropes. She is joined by two other females. The
three retrieve the nonsensical items from the clothesline, put
them on, and perform a spirited dance of celebration. "Obbligato"
returns to the lyrical mood of the opening. Two couples perform
lovely, simple lifts. The central figure, now subdued, rolls a
ball across the stage followed by another, then bounces one
playfully and throws it overhead. It does not come down.
After a pause, soap bubbles shimmer lazily down as the
lights slowly dim.

The whole work had somehow projected itself beyond
the proscenium, enveloping the audience with its evocative
images in a way that gave the tiny theater an indefinable "place
magic." *Another Touch of Klee* was the kind of Total Theater
which could only have evolved in a situation where the building
itself was an intrinsic part of the creative process.

Stan Kenton was pleased; audiences were pleased; critics
were delighted. People who came to see "Choreo '51" sometimes
came back to see the Klee-Kenton work again, bringing their
children. Albert Goldberg of the *Times*, now accepting bare feet,
found "a strongly Freudian aroma . . . but even if you can't
decipher the hidden meanings, the challenge is intriguing and the
patterns hold a good share of interest." Other critics, less
concerned with hidden meanings, were more lavish in their
praise.

Within a few days of the opening of "Choreo '51" the
Dance Theater Company was invited to appear at the Ojai Music
Festival a little more than a month off. This was the first time
that a dance group had ever been asked to participate in the
prestigious festival, which presented world-renowned musical
talents and attracted sophisticated and knowledgeable audiences
from throughout the Southwest. In the very short time available,
Horton, refreshed by the success of the new season, decided to
do a choreodrama based on the Robinson Jeffers version of
Medea. Judith Anderson was at the time playing to sold-out

houses throughout the United States in the title role and interest
was high in the well-known Greek legend.

Horton had been fascinated by the *deus ex machina* of
Greek tragic drama ever since he had read about it years before
while doing research for *Lysistrata.* To approximate symbolically
the ancient Greek stage machinery, he built his production using
filmic techniques such as the dissolve, the segue, the wipe, and
the flashback to effect his transitions between the eight scenes
of his scenario. One of his devices was the use of multiple
curtains. Medea pulls one aside to reveal and introduce other
main characters in the prologue; she draws another, just inside
the main curtain, to wipe out one scene; she swings (or rides) on
the second curtain; in the anguished climax she pulls a three-
foot-wide banner across the apron. The lights dim and the side
lighting reveals the children's bloody hand- and body-prints on
the fabric as insane laughter shrieks from the recorded score
and Medea performs what Carmen de Lavallade remembers as a
nearly impossibly difficult dance of madness while smoke rises
around her. The piece had been put together in too great a
hurry and was noticeably under-rehearsed at the first
performance. Like the choreography itself, the score by Audree
Covington had raw energy but lacked subtlety. The excellent
performances of Carmen de Lavallade, Rene De Haven, Jack
Dodds, James Truitte, and Vida Solomon somehow helped to
pull the production through, and it was a popular if not a
resounding critical success at Ojai. Horton took the whole thing
quite calmly, and a few weeks later proceeded to make small
revisions on the piece for performances at Dance Theater.
Still not at all satisfied, he wisely put it to rest at the
end of the season. He had explored several new ideas, of which
a few had worked well. This was enough; they would soon be
put to good use. If the choreography seemed strained and
refused to come into focus, this may have been because on a gut
level Horton was still too hurt by his own feelings of rejection

to be able to deal with the subject with artistic objectivity. His Medea raged almost from start to finish. Horton would never allow himself such emotionally excessive behavior in real life, and perhaps in this work he found some partial outlet for his anguish. He never spoke of reviving the piece.

The exciting possibility of an appearance at Mexico City's Palacio de Bellas Artes and El Patio Nightclub became a cause of great enthusiasm and more hard work at Dance Theater. The focus immediately went to building new repertory pieces, taking publicity photos, putting together an attractive brochure, and creating a whole new set of costumes. At almost the last moment, the venture fell through.

At about the same time, impresario Mary Bran flew to Paris to arrange a European tour for the group. When she arrived, she found that the Martha Graham Company had recently appeared quite unsuccessfully in the city and that modern dance was, for the time being, an anathema to her Parisian colleagues. Bran offered Horton a proposition similar to the one Sol Hurok had suggested over ten years earlier, but he could no more afford to put up funds now than he could in 1939. Another buildup and another disappointment.

During his lifetime, Horton's work was never seen outside of the United States. In the 1960s Alvin Ailey was responsible for presenting two Horton masterworks, *The Beloved* and *Dedication to José Clemente Orozco* in Europe and Asia. Both works were highly acclaimed by audiences and critics alike wherever they were shown.

Nineteen fifty-one was the most difficult year financially that Dance Theater was to know during Horton's lifetime. Both the children's school and the adult classes had been considerably diminished the previous year. At times the bank balance stood at pennies. During the summer run of "Choreo '51," in an effort to relieve the financial situation, Horton accepted an assignment to choreograph two musicals at the Greek Theater in Los Angeles,

Annie Get Your Gun and *Girl Crazy,* the former to have its
premiere at San Francisco's War Memorial Opera House. The
choice of Horton to do the choreography had not been
announced, and one of the male dancers who attended the
audition was a performer at Dance Theater who had promised to
appear in the entire summer "Choreo" season. He was auditioning
fully aware that conflicting time schedules made it impossible to
fulfill both commitments. Horton gave the boy the job knowing
that by so doing he had hired a valuable concert performer away
from himself. "How could I not have hired him," he later said,
looking miserable. "He was the best one there." Another dancer
would have to be found and taught the roles . . . extra
rehearsals . . . costumes . . . he knew the story by heart.

Before starting work on "Choreo '52" Horton set about
the arduous job of codifying his training techniques. He had
avoided formally consolidating this work for many years because
his was an ever-changing, ever-growing technique even within the
form it had been taking since the late 1930s. Now, perhaps
because of his ill health, Horton felt moved to tie his work
together. The undertaking involved setting eight semesters of
seventeen weeks of lesson plans. The work was started with
Louisa Kreck, Carmen de Lavallade, Kenneth Bartmess, and
George Allen, but soon others were drawn in. Horton's method
was crude, but he thought it workable. In work sessions he
would carefully set each exercise to counts and then assign
dancers to notate the movements as clearly as possible. At
the next work session, they were to teach the exercise from
their notes. When the results had been tested and approved, they
were recorded in notebooks. The objective was a book, richly
illustrated with photos, tentatively titled *The Basis of Modern
Dance.* Horton was probably projecting something on the order
of *Modern Dance, Techniques and Teaching** by Gertrude Shurr
and Rachael Yocom, a book he admired. There was also talk

*Gertrude Shurr and Rachael Yocom, *Modern Dance, Techniques and
Teaching* (New York: A.S. Barnes and Company, 1949).

about producing a film, if the necessary financing could be found. The project was never completed and the notes, so painstakingly recorded, are now worthless for reconstruction purposes. Too much had been left to the memory of the recorders, and years later, when they attempted to interpret them, it was to no avail. The careful work sessions did, however, prove to be of great value later in solidifying Horton's teaching techniques.

In late February and early March of 1952 Horton presented a series of performance-lectures in which he shared the results of his work on the codification with Dance Theater audiences. In the first half of the program he introduced techniques which he had named "Fortifications," "Deep Floor Vocabulary," "Dimensional Tonus," "Torso Language," "Pelvic Actions," "Hand-Foot-Face Vocabularies," "Fall Variations," "Aerial Vocabulary," and "Turn Motivations."

A good deal of the work was simply refinement and clarification of what he had developed with Lewitzky over several years. In addition to this considerable body of excellent teaching material, he had initiated a whole new range of movement ideas since her departure. Some of the newer movement material was abstracted from his recent choreographic excursions into ethnic sources, but now, rather than the gestures and postures he had utilized in his less mature years, it was the energy of the primitive that he captured and restated in his own terms. This is the eloquent Horton Technique which is being taught today.

In an effort to raise money for the Scholarship Fund, Horton and Eng somehow found the energy to stage the first of a series of "Bals Caribes," costume balls with a Caribbean Mardi gras-like atmosphere. In the first of these held at Dance Theater, in addition to entertainment by the Lester Horton Dancers, there was an art auction, and prizes were awarded for the best costumes. The event was so successful that the next year it was held at the spacious Los Angeles Breakfast Club.

Salome, 1950;
James Truitte,
Elle Johnson,
Carmen de Lavallade.
(Photo by
Charles Van Maanen.)

Workshop group on stage of Dance Theater, 1951.
(Dance Theater Collection.)

Lester Horton, 1952. (Photo by Constantine.)

Constantine

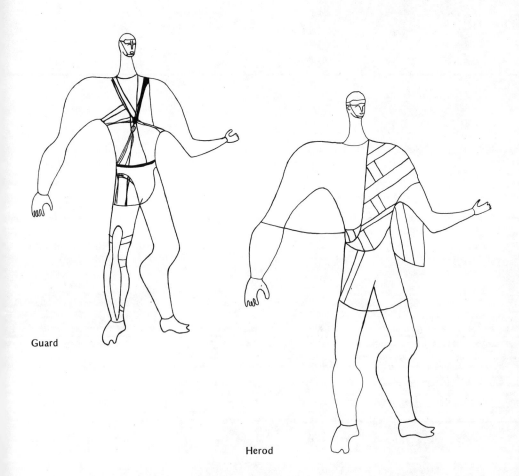

Guard

Herod

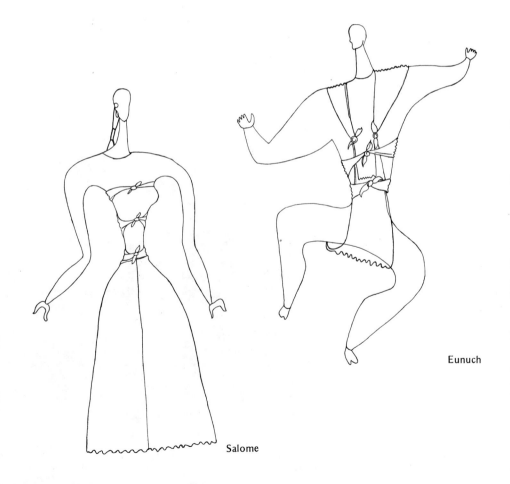

Salome sketches by Lester Horton, 1950.
(Dance Theater Collection.)

Eunuch

Salome

Another Touch of Klee, 1951;
Carmen de Lavallade, James Truitte, Lelia Goldoni.
(Photo by Constantine.)

Duke Ellington
at Dance Theater, 1952;
James Truitte,
Ellington,
Carmen de Lavallade,
Don Martin.
(Photo by Constantine.)

Liberian Suite, Rehearsal, 1952;
Alvin Ailey, Carmen de Lavallade in foreground.
(Photo by Charles Van Maanen.)

Liberian Suite, 1952;
Henry Dunn, Norman Cornick and chorus.
(Photo by Charles Van Maanen.)

Liberian Suite, 1952;
Joyce Trisler,
James Truitte,
Carmen de Lavallade.
(Photo by
Charles Van Maanen.)

For some time in the fall of 1950 Horton had thought of restaging his 1937 success, *Sacre du Printemps* at Dance Theater. The work on *Rhythm Section* for the 1950 mid-season program had been an invigorating return to his own sources, and he wanted to do a large work in this vein. However, a few weeks of the *Sacre* rehearsals convinced him that the Stravinsky work was not right for him at the time, and he let the idea rest. The 1951 season of "Fun Dances" rekindled his interest in making a major work which would be the culmination of his recent excursions into ethnic dance.

By a happy coincidence, Pat Willard, Duke Ellington's business manager, who was taking classes at Dance Theater, suggested to Horton that the composer-pianist's *Liberian Suite* would make an excellent score for choreography. Horton was enthusiastic and Ellington agreed. The two met, and what was supposed to be a half-hour business meeting turned into a three-hour chat. Ellington liked Horton and his Dance Theater and was impressed by the collection of percussion instruments which had become one of the most comprehensive on the West Coast. The visit with the talented, likeable musician was a tonic for Horton, and within a few days he was introducing new movement combinations into the teaching of his advanced classes. Company members always knew that a new work was being launched when a flood of unfamiliar technical materials suddenly appeared.

Ellington's *Liberian Suite* had been commissioned by the Liberian government in 1947 as part of that country's centennial celebration. The American première of the work was at Carnegie Hall in that year. Ellington conceived *Liberian Suite* as a series of five dances with rich primitive thematic material growing in sophistication from beginning to end. The work itself was a hybrid of popular and classical composition which could have been tailor-made for Horton's needs. It clearly defied pigeonholing in a way that he could deeply appreciate, having made many hybrid choreographic excursions of his own.

Working with great enthusiasm, Horton designed some of his finest costumes and accessories for *Liberian Suite.* He chose deep brown and red as his basic colors and created belts and hair ornaments of brass for the girls' costumes. For one section he constructed an ingenious skirt, mini-length, with broad raffia-trimmed panels attached to the hemline. One shoulder was left bare, creating a stunning, lush, asymmetrical line, which would look contemporary today. Weighted scarves were used both for their line and for the sound produced when they were beaten against the floor. The sets, too, revealed the gusto with which he was working. Large flats painted with free form human figures dressed the stage, and for the second section the rear studio was used as part of the dance space. Horton had stretched lengths of fabric, also figured, over the doors, creating a deep, cave-like illusion. In one section, two figures appeared at the most distant visible point in a spotlight and intertwined slowly in a series of breathtaking lifts and balances, somehow giving the impression of an approach from a great distance. Horton's choreography had an understated primitive elegance with bursts of joyous playfulness. The characteristic bearing of the upper body was the lifted open chest of the proud African tribesman, the head held with an eloquent sense of purpose. The movement phrases were long and rhythmically complex with an underlying sense of childlike naïveté about them. Modern, ethnic, and jazz motifs flowed together unselfconsciously. It was pure Horton and, as such, it was ahead of its time: too bold, too colorful, too physical for 1952. The music was purposely played very loudly to heighten the experience. Rock bands caught up with Horton a decade later on this idea.

If the critics failed to recognize the originality of the choreographic conception and the uniqueness of the costumes and decor, they were nonetheless pleased with the work. Albert Goldberg wrote in the *Los Angeles Times*:

> The dances are exuberant but not undisciplined, with
> African accents that were often exciting and always
> expertly realized by Miss de Lavallade, James Truitte and
> a large and vigorous company.

Many years later Alvin Ailey, who rehearsed in *Liberian Suite* but never performed in it, carried Horton's energetic and eloquent movement language, redefined through his own artistic sensibilities, to audiences throughout the world. The enthusiastic reception his work has received has been matched in dance only by performances of classical ballet's superstars. It has been estimated, and doubtless correctly, that the Ailey Dance Theater has been seen by more people than any other in the world. One television showing in the Soviet Union alone had a reported viewing audience of 22 million. He has done as much as any living person to popularize serious dance and build concert dance audiences, and one of his most important roots was his work with Lester Horton. From backstage viewings of *Barrel House* to rehearsals of *Liberian Suite*, it had been a vital apprenticeship.

In *7 Scenes With Ballabilli*, which opened "Choreo '52," Horton attempted to recreate some of the wild improvisational fun of the *commedia dell'arte*. However, the work seemed hastily put together, and the famous stock characters were not well differentiated. With lovely costumes by Eleanor Johnson, delightful props and masks, and a harlequin curtain strung between two pink ladders, the piece served its purpose, but not memorably.

One of Horton's finest achievements, *Prado de Pena*, with an excellent score by Gertrude Rivers Robinson and flawless choreographic craftsmanship, rounded out the program. In Garcia Lorca, Horton had found a writer who spoke to him as none ever had before, and the Spanish poet's *Yerma* struck a responsive chord. The work seemed to flow from him with

crystalline clarity as if it had been waiting to be born. Tragedy
was no longer a subject he could approach coolly as a theatrical
possibility as he had in *The Beloved*. Horton had survived the
loss of friends who were so close that they had become his
"family" and he had suffered a nearly fatal heart attack. In
Prado de Pena he was able to touch the heart of the tragic
mode for now he understood it, perhaps too well.

In telling this story of an unfulfilled marriage which
terminates in violence, Horton ingeniously divided his work into
sections by the entrance of three women, *jaleos*, fluttering
fans of various colors, and acting as a chorus. Frank Eng vividly
described *Prado de Pena* in an article for *Dance Perspectives*:

> *Prado de Pena* opens and closes on the barren one,
> surrounded by three *jaleo* figures. In the opening, Yerma
> is seated in a wicker chair, crooning over a non-existent
> infant she rocks in her arms, the *jaleo* figures hovering
> around in a flutter of solicitous fans. The first scene,
> 'Jaleo in Green — Yerma Dreams of Children,' starts as
> the trio moves out to rearrange three chairs on a diagonal.
>
> The setting revealed consists of a corral-like fence design,
> ominously draped with a voluminous black cloth and
> backdropped by Horton's own spray-painted gray, black,
> and white cyclorama depicting a gnarled and blasted tree
> stump.
>
> Yerma's solo flows into 'Jaleo in Green and Brown —
> Juan Dreams of Death,' wherein the impotent but jealous
> husband joins her in a lyric, reaching duet along the
> diagonal of chairs, which are rearranged by the chorus as
> Juan exits and Victor (the lover figure) enters for 'Jaleo
> in Pink and Vermilion — Victor Dreams of Spring.' Their
> ecstatic duo flows into 'Jaleo in Green and Yellow —
> Pagan Woman Offers Life.' In this mystical scene, the
> desperate Yerma consults a witch-woman, who presents
> her with the symbolic yellow figure of a child, leading

her into the 'Jaleo in Crimson and Yellow — Fertility
Ritual.' Here all the dancers but Yerma don masks to
take part in a strange, foot-pounding, rhythmic
incantation. At the climax of 'Jaleo in Black — Yerma
Bears a Child of Death,' the maddened Yerma strangles
Juan. The chorus pulls off the black cloth, revealing the
gaunt fence, and cover the act of murder. As the lights
dim, a series of gray death-masks are lowered from
overhead, and the chorus uncovers Yerma cradling the
dead Juan. The *jaleos* then return to Yerma with the
still-fluttering fans, again hovering around her as the lights
dim to black.

As was often the case with Horton's successful dramatic dances,
the ending of the piece was greeted by stunned silence.
        The role of Yerma was perfectly tailored to Carmen de
Lavallade, who had flowered into a splendid actress-dancer. In
her interpretation of the part, she combined strength and
lyricism, naïveté and agelessness, with a rare dramatic sensitivity.
It was a remarkable performance for a girl of twenty-one. The
fact of her youth was scarcely noted by critics, who were
unanimous in their praise. Fine performances were also delivered
by Richard D'Arcy, Norman Cornick, and Joyce Trisler, who at
seventeen played the pagan woman "who offers life" with great
clarity and assurance.
        During the season James Truitte stepped into the role of
Victor, and it became one of his best portrayals at Dance
Theater. One evening, just as he was to make his entrance in the
role, Horton stepped out of the shadows and whispered, "Dance
it with your balls." Afterwards, Lelia Goldoni, who knew
nothing of the incident, said to Truitte, "What happened?
You've never danced that well in your life!" The program
received excellent notices from the press and audiences flocked
to the most successful season since the first at the theater.
Increased enrollment at the school and good activity at the box

office had made the Dance Theater solvent again. Horton could at last take some pleasure in the knowledge that he had been able, with Frank Eng's help, to make Dance Theater work, in spite of poor health and financial problems.

Eng had done a great deal to make the success possible. From the time he took over the business management he had worked tirelessly to stabilize the venture financially by building audiences. Press books reveal that scarcely a week went by without some mention of the company in metropolitan newspapers. The Nisei press was kept up-to-date on Misaye Kawasumi's activities and, likewise, the black newspapers with news of de Lavallade and Truitte. Whenever a well-known personality came to visit the theater, Eng was sure to have a photographer there to record the event.

His introduction into the world of Dance Theater had come at a time when the bottom had fallen out of Horton's personal and professional life. The younger man's love for him, his seemingly limitless energy, and his enthusiasm for Dance Theater had helped Horton through the painful months before and after the dissolution and in the years since. However, the introduction of any strong new personality to a tightly-knit venture such as Dance Theater was bound to have attendant problems. Horton had become conciliatory and still tended to believe the best of people, even when he and his work were attacked. Eng, on the other hand, wishing to be protective, would throw himself between the attacker and his friend. The loyal young writer believed Horton to be a genius, and he faulted anyone who thought less of him. Horton's self-evaluation was somewhat different, and he requested that Eng no longer show up at rehearsals, not wishing to work under the pressure of so exalted an evaluation. During his best moments, he thought of Dance Theater as no more than the work he did: his job.

Carmelita Maracci, deeply impressed by *Prado de Pena*, told Horton that it was time to take his work to New York.

A hard and discerning critic, the brilliant teacher-choreographer
was not well known for praise and encouragement. Her own
exceptionally fine reputation had been established during two
decades of touring, dazzling audiences with her impassioned
dancing and choreography. She was deeply fond of Horton and
had much in common with him, for she also was a maverick
working in California. They had been dancing for the same
audiences and had suffered the same less-than-expert critics for
over twenty years. Out of her affection for him she gave special
attention to Dance Theater people in her incomparable ballet
classes, accepting no money from those who she knew could ill
afford to pay. Now she felt that Horton had reached a milestone
in his career with the Lorca piece and offered to help him with
contacts at the 92nd Street YM-YWHA in New York.

The "Y" was the logical place for the debut. For years,
under the direction of Dr. William Kolodney, it had provided a
showcase for dancers, poets, and musicians who needed a
medium-sized New York theater that was nominal in cost.
Maracci herself had performed there, and Janet Collins, whom
both she and Horton had trained, had been acclaimed four years
earlier at her East Coast debut on that stage.

Horton was ambivalent about going to New York. Three
years before it had seemed like a fine idea when Newell
Reynolds had tried without success to book a tour which was to
culminate in a New York appearance. Then, the company had
worked together for several years and had had many mature
performers: Rudi, Carl, Connie, Louisa, and Bella. Now there
were Carmen and Jimmy and a few others, but most of them
had much growing to do. On the other hand, battle-weary
though he was, Horton still wanted recognition from New York,
and especially from the *Times* critic John Martin, whom he
revered. It was a stimulating challenge. Frank Eng recalls,
"Horton did not approach the trip starry-eyed or expecting his
name to become a household word overnight. I think
fundamentally he saw it as a logical step in the growth of the

company." He would be putting his reputation on the line with that young group, but he had done that year in and year out for nearly twenty-five years. Horton and Eng, encouraged by the success of "Choreo '52" and Maracci's enthusiasm, contacted the "Y" and were accepted for a two-performance appearance the following March.

Money for the venture was, of course, a problem. In the 1930s it had cost between $200 and $300 to mount a full presentation of the Lester Horton Dance Group. Now the cost was ten times that much. Expenses for the upkeep of Dance Theater were very high, and Horton counted a break-even year as a good one. At the age of 47 his assets and liabilities were about equal, an accountant's euphemism for being "dead broke." With perfect timing, however, a movie assignment came along, and this made the venture possible. Producer Sol Lesser signed Horton to choreograph and direct a segment of *3-D Follies*, to be known as "Caribbean Nights" (encore "Frevo" and "Cumbia"). The assignment meant good pay for the dancers and a little over $2000 net to Horton. The projected budget for the trip, which included transporting, housing and feeding twelve people and shipping the large *Salome* set, was $500 to $700 more than that. Eng immediately tried to arrange a few concert bookings along the way, but he was too late for the current booking season, and one date in Chicago on the return trip was to prove considerably more trouble than it was worth. Optimistically, Horton and Eng believed that, even at the barest minimum, box office receipts from the three scheduled performance dates would net them enough to make up the deficit.

Early in March, "Choreo '53" had its premiere at the Wilshire-Ebell Theater in an effort to improve the group's financial situation. The program, which also served as a dress rehearsal for New York, included *7 Scenes With Ballabilli*, a revival of *The Beloved*, Horton's fifth and final revival of

Salome (now called *Face of Violence*), and the première of
Dedications in Our Time.

Although a few of the dedications were flawed by
Horton's old problem of choreographic attenuation, at least one
authentic masterwork came out of the group, and several had
sections which won high praise from critics on both coasts. The
dedication "To Ruth [St. Denis], Mary [Wigman] and Martha
[Graham]" might have been saved by remembering Doris
Humphrey's well-known admonition, "All dances are too long."
There were, nevertheless, breathtaking balances and moments of
soaring lyricism. It was a generous attempt by Horton to
acknowledge a debt of gratitude to these three creative giants of
modern dance. Joyce Trisler recalls an amusing incident which
took place at a 1954 audition for Doris Humphrey, who had not
been included in Horton's tribute. Unaware that Martha Graham
and Miss Humphrey were not on the best of terms at the time,
Trisler chose her own role in the trio, the dedication to Martha,
for her audition material. Only later did she discover why the
great choreographer, who was later to become her friend and
teacher, had watched the dance with such an odd expression.

"To Carson McCullers" proved to be almost painfully
sentimental and was retired after three performances. The
"Memorial to Hiroshima" was timely in 1952 and, though
wickedly difficult and overly long, beautifully conceived and
performed. Tiny Misaye Kawasumi, clad in white, the Japanese
color of mourning, was given 10 minutes of precarious knee
crawls and swirls in which her upper body was seldom more
than a few feet off the ground. The solo was never performed
by another dancer, because it required a duplication of the
flexibility, endurance, thigh strength, and physical proportions
of the talented young Nisei's body. Horton had created it
especially for her.

In all of his creative years, Horton had never made a
dramatic work in which the male was the most important

central figure. He had choreographed stunning movement for
men, but always to set off a female protagonist to greater
advantage. Now, in the dedication "To Federico Garcia Lorca,"
which he choreographed for James Truitte, he unconsciously
crafted a self-portrait. In this work the central figure is isolated,
yet clearly conscious of the other dancers and his audience as he
explores the stage space. At one point, dancers enter with two
thirty-foot lengths of fabric and form a cross on the stage floor.
The Lorca figure stands in the center in a plane of loneliness. At
the conclusion he is surrounded by three women fluttering fans,
walking forward into the oncoming darkness. Frank Eng, for
one, felt that Horton had choreographed his own epitaph.

The dedication to "José Clemente Orozco" represents
Horton at his best, and is one of the authentic gems of the
modern dance repertory. The music was a reuse of the score
Kenneth Klaus had created for "Soldadera." Characteristically,
Horton put a good score to good use more than once. Years of
exploration of the Mexican psyche and passion for freedom,
dating as far back as the 1935 *Mound Builders,* had gone into
the preparation of this splendid work which, fortunately, has
been preserved and is being performed today by groups headed
by James Truitte, Alvin Ailey, Joyce Trisler, and Mary Anthony.
Deborah Jowitt described James Truitte's revival of this work
in a 1973 *Village Voice* review of a performance by the
Cincinnati Ballet Company:

> Dedication to José Clemente Orozco is my favorite Horton
> dance of those I've seen—simple, strong, vived. It shows a man
> and a woman, Mexican peasants, both wearing bandoliers,
> marching. During the whole duet, they march—swaying from
> side to side, advancing, falling, retreating, advancing They
> stare at invisible oppressors. Occasionally they help and support
> each other. For one retreat, he crawls away with her lying on
> his back, rolling off, rolling back on. It's one of the most eloquent
> and stylish protest dances I've ever seen.

In *Face of Violence* Horton skillfully combined the compressed emotion of the Noh play, in which time is used symbolically, with the wildness and exaggeration of Kabuki and a touch of the Grand Guignol. All were shaped by his considerable abilities as a storyteller and staged with consummate theatricality. Here the attenuation was purposeful, for the slow pace of the narrative heightened the power of the grisly climax. There is nothing else quite like it in the modern dance repertory.

A critic later wrote about the production:

> ... It may seem hard to believe that in this day and age it is still possible to engender intense excitement by telling once again, the well-worn legend of the apocryphal Salome. Such was the effect of the *Face of Violence*, however. Carmen de Lavallade's Salome is an altogether remarkable conception — passionate, childishly capricious, lascivious, with a sheer physical beauty that compels a fascinated attention from the moment of her entry in her splendid gold and black gown, cinctured with gold, a fan held coquettishly against her cheek. The pas de deux in which she seduces the guard, a magnificent figure as portrayed by Jack Dodds, is an extraordinary piece of theatrical invention. Joyce Trisler makes Herodias a termagant in a whirlwind of fury, and James Truitte catches exactly the mixture of lechery and vacillating weakness which is the traditional idea of Herod.

A week after the Wilshire-Ebell performance, two station wagons were loaded with sets, props, costumes, and people—six to a car. Suitcases and set pieces were carefully lashed to the roofs and covered by tarpaulins. On board were Horton, Eng, Carmen de Lavallade, Lelia Goldoni, Misaye Kawasumi, Joyce Trisler, James Truitte, Norman Cornick, Val Goodrich, Jack Dodds, Lelia's mother, and costume mistress Martha Koerner. As they made their way southeast on the Hollywood Freeway, they

must have borne more than a passing resemblance to another car
that had headed west in 1928.

   Midway through the trip, after a 14-hour driving day, a
motel refused to accommodate the interracial company.
Fortunately that happened only once during the cross-country
trek, and that was a good record for 1953.

Lester Horton conducting rehearsal, 1952.
(Photo by Bob Willoughby.)

Prado de Pena, 1952;
Norman Cornick, Joyce Trisler,
Richard D'Arcy, Carmen de Lavallade (kneeling).
(Photo by Charles Van Maanen.)

Prado de Pena, 1952;
Henry Dunn, Norman Cornick, and chorus.
(Photo by Charles Van Maanen.)

Prado de Pena, 1952;
Carmen de Lavallade, Norman Cornick. (Photo by Charles Van Maanen.)

Lester Horton, Lelia Goldoni, 1952.
(Photo by Charles Van Maanen.)

new york

On March 24, 1953, the troupe arrived in New York exhausted and cramped from having been packed together like sardines for six days. Horton and Eng wondered where the dancers found the energy when they happily took off on a boat ride around Manhattan after the first full day of rehearsal. Only the night before, they had claimed to be on death's doorstep from fatigue. The sets were painstakingly and expensively duplicated to comply with union regulations, and the dancers familiarized themselves with the new theater space while Horton adjusted the choreography. Although the seating capacity of the Kaufmann Auditorium at the "Y" was many times that of Dance Theater, the stage space was *twelve feet* shallower!

During the four days of preparation it became apparent that advance publicity had been less than adequate. Of the New York dance critics, only Walter Terry had informed his readers that the California dancers were to appear at the "Y." The event was in competition with an upcoming two-week modern dance festival under the sponsorship of the B. de Rothschild Foundation. Martha Graham, Doris Humphrey, José Limón, and Merce Cunningham were among the luminaries whose work would be shown. Eng got busy trying to publicize the concert, but lacking professional contacts and without funds for advertising there was little he could do. As they had feared, attendance was poor. Only 300 tickets had been sold for the Saturday night performance and 200 for the Sunday matinee; but those who came cheered.

Lester Horton was no longer an obscure California choreographer in the eyes of the modern dance "establishment." Under the most difficult circumstances he had shown his work in New York at last, and poor attendance notwithstanding, he had been successful. He had paved the way for further appearances of his dancers and left quite a few knowledgeable people with the feeling that they had seen something novel and refreshing.

He had reason to be proud of his courageous accomplishment; yet even this small triumph was marred by dismay at the size of the audiences and concern about financing the trip home. William Kolodney assured the somewhat depressed and worried choreographer and his business manager that the unbridled enthusiasm of the audience reception was unusual and easily equal to that received by Carmelita Maracci and Janet Collins in their respective New York debuts. But this was small consolation, considering their problems, and for several days there would be no reviews to console them.

Nevertheless, there were a few pleasant surprises for Horton. Kita van Cleve, a special favorite of his from the Horton Dance Group days, had heard of the concert and was full of words of praise for his current work. Stanley Haggart, an old friend, gave a reception for the dancers. Margaret Lloyd, who had written a comprehensive article about his work in her *Borzoi Book of Modern Dance*,* complimented him warmly on the performances. A few days later she wrote in the *Christian Science Monitor:*

> Out of an embracive cultural background come
> choreographies of wide spatial values, voluminous spiral

*Margaret Lloyd, *The Borzoi Book of Modern Dance* (New York: Alfred A. Knopf, Inc., 1949).

> turns, horizontal swoopings across the floor, oblique
> swervings and circlings over an assortment of stage
> levels . . . Now the torso leans backward or sideward
> from the knees at an impossible angle and suddenly goes
> off in another tangent. The movement is broad and
> sustained . . . it unfolds with logical unpredictability.

Elsewhere in the article she notes with appreciation his careful integration of costume, decor, music, and sound effects. Horton must have smiled at Lloyd's enthusiastic summing up of *Prado de Pena*. "The movement is pregnant," she wrote, "with the drama of sterility." With his love of one-liners, he might have wished he had said that first.

Much as he would have liked to, Horton could not afford to keep the group in New York to wait for reviews. They drove on to Chicago, using Frank Eng's vacation pay, which he had wisely taken along. After sizing up the financial situation there, it became obvious that help was needed if they were ever to get home, and Horton wired his agent Jessie Kulberg for a $300 loan. She kindly sent twice that amount, her full commission for the *3-D Follies* job.

Horton, feeling somehow that he had failed in New York and upset by yet another financial setback, began to drink more heavily and openly. Eng tried to dissuade him, but this always led to unpleasantness between them and finally he stopped trying. There were other factors feeding this dependency: minor tensions in the group, concern about the immediate future of Dance Theater, and always the fear of death, which was never far from Horton's thoughts.

When the little caravan reached Gallup, New Mexico, in spite of his fatigue and ill health, Horton insisted on taking his young charges for a visit to the Navajo trading post outside the city. As the dancers moved about in a light early-morning snowfall, the Indians seemed as interested in the motley collection of races as the visitors were in them. Frank Eng later wrote, "We knew those dark-eyed, aristocratic, pastel-hatted Indians were staring holes through us, but try as we might, we never caught one of them looking." It was a memorable adventure with Horton leading the way, explaining some of the unfamiliar crafts and giving advice on modest purchases of silver and turquoise. He seemed happier and more relaxed than he had been in years.

When the reviews caught up with them in Los Angeles, there was some reason to rejoice. Walter Terry had written a warm and friendly review, a welcome to New York to an important artist who had waited a long time to get there:

> The Lester Horton Dancers . . . brought vigor and polish, and imagination to their programs at the Y.M. and Y.W.H.A. . . . Mr. Horton's choreography and his staging of it was wholeheartedly theatrical. Dramatic development, dynamic contrasts, movement surprises and clear expositions of plot or mood or joke were, with few exceptions, maintained throughout the program . . . the local debut of the Lester Horton Dancers gave cause for pride in the modern dance efforts of Californians and brought freshness of idea, new faces, fine dancing, theatrical verve and even, perhaps, a healthy dash of envy to New Yorkers who attended.

The opening paragraphs of Doris Hering's review in *Dance Magazine* were neither warm nor friendly. At the outset she dismissed Horton as a reflector rather than an innovator, and told her readers that he was not a pioneer to be classed with Doris Humphrey and Martha Graham. "His dances appeal to the eye more than to the heart," she wrote, complaining about the general lack of integration of the emotional and the pictorial. Of *Prado de Pena,* she described "variations full of flavor and atmosphere—variations more kaleidoscopic in their melting patterns than inexorable with the hidden pulse of true tragedy."

She gives only the duet *To José Clemente Orozco* her grudging approval. However, she found the company delightful, "with the similarity of energy output and body alignment that comes only from working together over a period of time. . . ." She continued:

> Miss de Lavallade is a find. Tall, lithe, seemingly lyric in attack, she is also capable of wide emotional range and sustained dramatic concentration. And like all the Horton dancers, she performs with a devotion that admirably reflects the atmosphere in which she has been trained.

P. W. Manchester's review in *Dance News* was splendid:

> After twenty-five years of hearsay reports, and speculation based on the quality of such dancers as Janet Collins and James Mitchell, New York finally had an opportunity to see the Lester Horton Dancers for itself, and it can be said at once that New York was not only deeply impressed but (possibly) a little humbled.
>
> These dancers are terrific both as individuals and as a company. They are completely unselfish in their subordination to the discipline of the group. Every work is presented with a passionate attention to the last detail of movement, costuming, decor, and lighting, and the musical scores by Gertrude Rivers Robinson, are exceptionally interesting in their affinity to the works for which they were composed.

Although he had been in the audience, the much hoped for review from John Martin did not come. This was a deep disappointment, and Horton was never to learn that Mr. Martin was, at the time, limiting his reviews to concerts in major Broadway theaters. Another first-rate talent of Horton's generation, a man deeply interested in Total Theater of another genre, Alwin Nikolais, had to wait several years for a review from that influential dance critic.

The "Y" performances led to a warm invitation from
Ted Shawn for the group to open the program at Jacob's Pillow
the following summer. In 1952, Shawn's wife, Ruth St. Denis,
had visited Dance Theater. She later said, "I was very impressed
with that lovely little theater and the classes there. His
movement techniques are tough but they are marvelous. But
when I saw the performance. . . ." She shrugged her shoulders
and went on, "Dance should be a balance between here, here,
and here. . . ." She pointed to her head, her heart, and then her
pelvis. "Too much of here." She pointed to her pelvis again.
"You know what I mean?"

After returning to Los Angeles, Eng noticed with genuine
alarm how ill Horton looked and decided that regardless of their
financial condition they could no longer continue to live in the
studio. The Horton share of the Chatsworth house had been
bought out by Bill and Portia Bowne several years earlier, and
the elder Hortons were living in a rustic wooded canyon in
Woodland Hills on the opposite side of the San Fernando
Valley. Now, to make the purchase of a home possible, it was
decided to consolidate households. Once again a film assignment,
Horton's 19th, came to the rescue. This was Warner Brothers'
South Sea Woman, starring Virginia Mayo and Burt Lancaster.
Horton choreographed a Tahitian wedding dance which James
Truitte remembers as outstanding. Unfortunately, most of it was cut
from the finished film.

Horton and Eng found, nestled in the Hollywood Hills, a
modest frame and stucco house which could be reached only by
a precariously steep driveway. The view from the living room
was of rugged, unspoiled hillsides covered with chaparral,
tumbleweed, and patches of cactus. To the west one could see
for miles, and spectacular sunsets were commonplace. In that
surprisingly wild area it was easy at night to imagine being in
the desert or on the prairie. The dark canyon canopied by stars

and the sounds of nocturnal creatures chirping and buzzing did
not contradict the fantasy. These were sounds Horton knew and
loved. In his spare moments he did some gardening, and in just a
few months he had a few dozen varieties of cactus growing in
the narrow patio outside the living room. Poly Anna and Iredell,
now in their 70s, were content with the quiet remoteness of the
house, and they liked being close to their son. They watched
television a great deal and kept the place tidy. For once it was a
blessing to have them around. Horton could concentrate on
moving plants about, and he spent a few minutes now and then
watching the animals scurry about on the warm hillside.

One of Horton's closest personal friends, the
photographer and author Constantine Hassalevris, remembers
that at this time Horton became involved in a near tragedy. A
young black dancer who was working his way up in the Dance
Theater ranks was accused of rape and thrown into jail. He had
made the mistake of being in a South Bay beach resort at the
time the alleged rape was committed and was arrested for the
crime. The hysterical victim had positively identified him as her
assailant. Knowing that the youngster, a polite and gentle boy,
was incapable of committing the crime, Horton sprang into
action, collecting character references from every prominent
person he knew. One, a friend in public relations work, refused
to help. The McCarthy investigations were at their height, and
he was afraid of becoming involved in such a *liberal* cause.
Horton was dumbfounded. For a while he was silent, his face
becoming paler as his eyes watered. Then in a rare rage he cried
out, "Damn it to Hell!" and wept as no one had ever seen him
weep in his adult life. He redoubled his efforts and at last the
young man was released. Within a month the victim *positively*
identified two other assailants.

Frank Eng made excellent use of the fine reviews from
New York to help publicize "Choreo '53" at Dance Theater.

The season went well, and the appearance at Jacob's Pillow had been successful enough to lead to an invitation for a return visit the following summer. As an economy measure neither Horton nor Eng had gone along on the trip.

Most of the late summer was spent settling into the new house and preparing for the third fund-raising "Bal Caribe." This was to be the largest and most spectacular fund raiser of them all. Arrangements were made to reopen the defunct Earl Carroll's supper club. Horton exhausted himself staging ten dances, many of them new, for the event. The "Bal" was successful beyond all expectations. It had become the costume event of the year, attracting a large assortment of people, from show business hopefuls to shop girls, all costumed to the teeth, as well as others who had come only to look.

As a result of the brilliant success of the "Bal," the Horton Dancers were booked into the then world-famous Ciro's Night Club. For Horton this engagement represented an important moral victory. Until this time, offers to place the group had stipulated that Horton send all Black, Oriental, or white performing units. He had steadfastly refused, closing the door to prestigious bookings, not only in Hollywood but in Las Vegas as well. He insisted that anyone who hired his company should be willing to take the gamble that night club audiences were as ready to accept an interracial dance group as Dance Theater audiences had been. Ciro's had taken that gamble, and now the way was open for the Horton Dancers and other interracial groups to perform in both cities.

Horton was busy once more with strenuous rehearsals, now carrying a can of beer with him whenever he rehearsed or taught. In a 1975 interview, Joyce Trisler remembered that the happy working atmosphere at Dance Theater was undiminished by Horton's heavy drinking.

> Even in his bad times there was a tremendous sense of fun
> and good spirits around the place. Lester projected a total

joy in the work. His classes were always filled with
humor. He was very bawdy and the comments he made
were sometimes outrageous. It wasn't what he said that
was particularly memorable but his timing and the fact
that he said something like that at all. Often it was a
one-liner that he whispered to you as he walked by . . .
We all worked with such deep concentration and his
humor was our escape valve. We learned to laugh at him
and at ourselves.

His relationship with these youngsters had become warm
and intimate. As in the past, working closely with Horton meant
acquiring a new family, and this group, several of whom were
fatherless or motherless, willingly accepted him as a loving parent
figure. His heart attack and subsequent illness had mellowed him
and increased his perceptiveness and, his personal problems
notwithstanding, the role of patriarch fit him admirably. Days
off from work at the theater were often spent at the new house
in the hills, with Horton and Eng preparing sumptuous meals
and members of the company visiting together as friends. Trisler
recalled:

The master/pupil thing did not exist with us. Lester did
not want or need the kind of ritual I found later in the
New York dance scene. On the contrary, we were a
bunch of renegade kids and would talk back to him all
the time. He seemed to encourage our independence. He
was nurturing us and opening our minds to literature,
music, politics, painting, costume design, and choreography. We were bombarded and challenged constantly.
He opened a world to us.

Near the end of the interview Trisler sat quietly for a
moment and then spoke, choosing her words carefully:

> We were very young, and I was very intense . . . neurotic
> as hell, actually . . . I was always causing problems. I was
> thrown out of the company on one occasion. One
> evening during a rehearsal break I collapsed in one of the
> chairs of *The Beloved* set in the back corner of the
> studio. A few minutes later, Lester walked over to me
> and looked at me as if he were looking into me. Then he
> said, 'I hope you know how much I love you.' I was
> surprised and made some sarcastic remark; suddenly he
> was gone. Later when I told people he had said that to
> me, they didn't believe me. We were all very close but
> Lester never spoke like that. . . .

The following day he cheerfully asked the devoted secretary of the school, Lilyan Silver, who was on her way to do some shopping, to pick up a wild shirt for him if she spotted one. On November 1, Ciro's picked up the option on the dance group for an additional two weeks. Notices had been excellent. The next morning Lester Horton died of a heart attack in his home on Mulholland Drive. He was 47.

A few days later John Martin wrote in the *New York Times*:

> The death of Lester Horton of a heart attack last week
> comes as a great shock to those who have taken it for
> granted that he would always be at work on the West
> Coast, supplying creative activity and energy and living
> support to the dance at the other edge of the country.
> Certainly he has been a tower of strength to the modern
> dance for twenty years, and his mark has been put
> indelibly upon it.

author's note

Frank Eng was able to keep the doors of Dance Theater open for seven years after Horton's death. He produced several seasons of dance performed by both the adult concert group and Dance Theater II, comprised of talented youngsters at the Dance Theater School. During this period, Alvin Ailey made his first important attempts at choreography and James Truitte came into his full maturity as a performer and teacher. Both Truitte and Carmen de Lavallade were to be featured dancers in the Alvin Ailey Dance Theater company in the 1960s, performing throughout the United States and in Southeast Asia and Australia.

notes and sources

abbreviations

IMJ	Isabel Morse Jones writing in the *Los Angeles Times*.
V.H. (S)	Viola Hegyi (Swisher) writing in *Hollywood Citizen News*.
D.P.	Larry Warren, Frank Eng, Bella Lewitzky, and Joyce Trisler, *Dance Perspectives* 31: *The Dance Theater of Lester Horton*, Autumn, 1967.
Tape	Tape recorded interview.
Interview	Interview not recorded on tape.

a regional theater is born

page

5	"He had this strange ability. . . ." Tape: Toni Masarachia, August 8, 1973, Laguna Beach, California.
9	"Horton's passionate studies. . . ." Walter Hickman, *Indianapolis Times*, December 14, 1934.
11	"Give us a theater. . . ." Quoted in *Booth Tarkington Civic Theater Golden Anniversary Yearbook*, 1964.
16	"One of the most impressive. . . ." Doane-Holtzman, *Indianapolis News*, July 5, 1926.
17	"in the interests. . . ." Publicity flyer dated October 12, 1928.
19	"strikingly beautiful. . . ." *Indianapolis News*, November 11, 1927.

young man goes west

page

22   "I regard Mr. Horton. . . ." Program for Dance Repertory Group
        dated August 28, 1931.
23   " 'Mama' came religiously. . . ." Tape: Katherine Stubergh Keller,
        May 24, 1967, Los Angeles.
23   "The words were Longfellow's. . . ." Redfern Mason, *San Francisco
        Examiner,* May 11, 1929.
26   "He had a large variety. . . ." Tape: Elsie Martinez, July 11, 1973,
        Carmel, California.
29   "My memories go back. . . ." Letter dated September 27, 1939.
30   "Lester read. . . ." Tape: Katherine Stubergh Keller, May 24,
        1967, Los Angeles.
32   "In the early 1930s. . . ." Tape: Keller.
33   "Lester was always digging. . . ." Tape: Keller.
34   "I can scarcely remember. . . ." Interview: Jean Abel, May 15,
        1967, Santa Barbara, California.
36   "Lester gave. . . ." Tape: Karoun Tootikian, June 12, 1970, Los
        Angeles.
41   "We felt that. . . ." Bella Lewitzky, D.P. p. 48.

salome dances

page

45   "It was as if. . . ." Interview: Elizabeth Talbot-Martin, April 10,
        1967, North Hollywood, California.
49   "more interesting as a promise. . . ." IMJ, August 9, 1934.
50   "He did not dance. . . ." Bella Lewitzky, D.P. p. 47.
50   "He was a most imperfect. . . ." William Bowne, in a note to the
        author, November, 1975.
51   "imbued with dramatic strength. . . ." IMJ, July 26, 1934.
51   "His grasp of elemental. . . ." Florence Lawrence, *Los Angeles
        Examiner,* December 1, 1934.
51   "It had moments. . . ." W.E. Oliver, *Los Angeles Examiner,*
        August 9, 1934.
51   "Too many different ideas. . . ." IMJ, August 9, 1934.
51   "The modern dance. . . ." VH(S), July 26, 1934.
52   "If this is truly. . . ." Article from Lester Horton's personal
        scrapbook; name of publication and by-line are missing.

page

54   "Once you've seen him. . . ." Vernon Carter, *Los Angeles Record*,
        December 1, 1934.
54   "There is a need. . . ." Dorathi Bock Pierre, *American Dancer*,
        February, 1936.
55   "This daring, unconventional. . . ." W. E. Oliver, *Los Angeles
        Herald and Express*, December 1, 1934.
55   " 'Dance to Zapata'. . . ." Juan André, *Script*, March, 1935.

dancers unite!

page

57   "a national organization. . . ." Program for New Dance League,
        dated March 21, 1936.
57   "We must express. . . ." *New York Post*, October 16, 1936.
59   "Dancing reflects social. . . ." *New York Post*, October 16, 1936.
63   "It was the noisiest. . . ." Tape: Bella Lewitzky, June 28, 1967, Los
        Angeles.
64   "If he felt a criticism. . . ." Tape: Lewitzky.
66   "I am sincerely. . . ." Dorathi Bock Pierre, *American Dancer*,
        October, 1937.
66   "This man is going. . . ." Joyce Trisler, D.P. p. 64
69   "No one ever. . . ." Bella Lewitzky, D.P. p. 53
71   "My first introduction. . . ." Tape: Bella Lewitzky for her
        company, February 3, 1967, Los Angeles.
72   "We . . . believe. . . ." *Theater Journal* (Los Angeles), February,
        1936.
74   "He would try. . . ." Tape: Bella Lewitzky for her company,
        February 3, 1967, Los Angeles.
76   "*Chronicle* is a. . . ." Program dated January 17, 1937.
79   "In Ku Klux Klan. . . ." Bella Lewitzky, D.P. p. 49.
80   "In the general. . . ." Margaret Lloyd, *The Borzoi Book of Modern
        Dance* (New York: Alfred A. Knopf, Inc., 1949. Republished, New
        York: Dance Horizons), p. 278 (pagination as in the Dance
        Horizons edition).
80   "showed a pioneer. . . ." *Ibid.*, p. 289.
80   "There is some. . . ." *Ibid.*, p. 279.
81   "Salome is a remarkably. . . ." W. E. Oliver, *Los Angeles Herald and
        Express*, April 27, 1937.
81   "In the concluding. . . ." Helen King, *Dance Magazine*, June, 1937.

page
82   "They are a dozen. . . ." IMJ, April 4, 1937.
84   "The modern realism. . . ." IMJ, August 6, 1937.
84   "One word describes. . . ." Dorathi Bock Pierre, *American Dancer*, October, 1937.
85   "Lester Horton's choreo-drama. . . ." IMJ, October 2, 1937.
86   "Eventually modern. . . ." Alfred Frankenstein, *San Francisco Chronicle*, April 25, 1938.
93   "Blossoming out in. . . ." From Lester Horton's personal scrapbook; name of publication and by-line are missing.
95   "The Horton Dance Group. . . ." IMJ, November 5, 1939.
97   "With the same. . . ." VH(S), February 3, 1941.
98   "Everyone loved to work. . . ." Interview: Herman Boden, August 25, 1970, Reseda, California

interlude

page
110   "denatured *Oklahoma!*" Lloyd, p. 282.
112   "Yes, but I. . . ." Bella Lewitzky, D.P. p. 86.

dance theater

page
120   "He accompanied himself. . . ." Bella Lewitzky, D.P. p. 52.
124   "There is a good. . . ." Albert Goldberg, *Los Angeles Times*, undated clipping.
125   "Never handy at. . . ." Goldberg, undated clipping.
125   "The inescapable and. . . ." Frank Eng, *Los Angeles Daily News*, June 16, 1948.
126   "It was with no. . . ." Frank Eng interviewed in *Los Angeles Tribune*, April 30, 1954.
135   "When his work became. . . ." Tape: William Bowne, June 13, 1974, San Diego, California.
138   "We are fortunate. . . ." Lecture Demonstration notes, dated February 27, 1952.
138   "Running close to her. . . ." Darr Smith, *Los Angeles Daily News*, January 30, 1950.
139   "In 'Frevo' the enthusiasm. . . ." Miriam Geiger, *Los Angeles Tribune*, February 4, 1950. (In Lewitzky's scrapbook numerous lines in the review are underlined.)

page

143   "Lester taught me how. . . ." Tape: Carmen de Lavallade, July 2,
       1975, New York City.
143   "To Carmen de Lavallade. . . ." *Dance Magazine*, May, 1967.
144   "Long ago, Lester Horton. . . ." *Ibid.*

rebuilding

page

148   "Choreo '51 marks a. . . ." Dance Theater program dated 1951.
151   "When the curtain opened. . . ." Tape: James Truitte, June 3,
       1973, New York City.
153   "a strongly Freudian. . . ." Albert Goldberg, *Los Angeles Times*,
       April 2, 1951.
156   "How could I not. . . ." Tape: Constantine Hassalevris, August
       15, 1970, Los Angeles.
167   "The dances are exuberant. . . ." Albert Goldberg, *Los Angeles
       Times*, March 26, 1952.
168   *"Prado de Pena. . . ."* Frank Eng, D.P. pp. 40-41.
174   "Dedication to José. . . ." Deborah Jowitt, *Village Voice*,
       August 30, 1973.
175   "It may seem. . . ." P. W. Manchester, *Dance News*, May, 1953.

new york

page

182   "Out of an embracive. . . ." Margaret Lloyd, *Christian Science
       Monitor* (Boston) April 4, 1953.
184   "The Lester Horton Dancers. . . ." Walter Terry, *New York
       Herald Tribune*, April 5, 1953.
185   "Miss de Lavallade. . . ." Doris Hering, *Dance Magazine,* May, 1953.
185   "After twenty-five years. . . ." P. W. Manchester, *Dance News,*
       May, 1953.
186   "I was very impressed. . . ." Ruth St. Denis, in a conversation
       with the author, Summer, 1952.
188   "Even in his. . . ." Tape: Joyce Trisler, June 26, 1975, New York
       City.
189   "The master/pupil thing. . . ." Tape: Trisler.
190   "We were very young. . . ." Tape: Trisler.
190   "The death of. . . ." John Martin, *New York Times*, November 8,
       1953.

for the record

Grammar, punctuation, and spelling in this section are reproduced unaltered from original sources.

horton on dance

AN OUTLINE APPROACH TO CHOREOGRAPHY

It is essential to define a new point of concentration in teaching choreography. The day of generalizing in pre-classic dance forms, dancing bleakly in practice costumes in a bare uncompromising studio may draw fittingly to its end.

Choreography should be approached in a richer environment. The modern dance has discovered its inherent theater and the implications are being realized on every hand—handsome wardrobe, more varied accompaniment, the spoken word, immediate contemporary meanings, scenic investiture. The choreography of a dynamic dance cannot remain unchanging. It grows yearly more lucid, more versatile, more compelling.

Education lags behind the advanced professional accomplishment. This cannot be avoided, but the lag should be shortened as much as possible. Instruction in choreography should reflect the tendency of current works. It should find the student in a three dimensional environment, rich with sculptural masses, employing color and light in a significant way, utilizing the effectiveness of costume to enrich movement and meaning, and conceiving accompaniment and program note as a fully clarified expression from the beginning. Above all, the dance should be carefully and fully documented. That is the important thing, the factor which changes choreography from improvisation to composition, which raises a variation to the level of a development.

Lester Horton, *Educational Dance, Vol. 3,* No. 3 (August-September) 1940.

Every teacher (every dancer, indeed) is familiar with the utter inadequacy the student feels when he is asked to invent movement. Anyone with decent humility is sure to be confounded by the request. When the problem is to improvise, the reaction is still more general and pronounced. And how this reaction impedes growth in the dance composer! Free fantasy is a priceless attribute which we sell in exchange for a stodgy education during our childhood. Imagination is exchanged for rationality. We need them both to compose. The gift for fantasy, for a free invention of movement, must be regained.

We have tried many devices in the last years, improvising to music which was rich in suggestion because of its mature form, developing a group mood to set aside inhibitions, relying on the strong insistence of percussion accompaniment, borrowing from the primitives, leaning on the pre-classic forms. Each of these reached a few people, developed a few dancers past the initial stages of movement making. Gradually improving teaching attitudes successfully have drawn out even retiring students. But the results are still mediocre.

Now, however, the question is clarifying itself. It becomes clear as the advanced choreographers speak more pointedly of wide objective meanings in the idiom of the dance that if you have something to say you will find the means of saying it. For the student of dance-composition this means that the content closest to him, not the elusive emotion, not the abstract form, but the substantial realities about which he can conduct a serious objective investigation shall be the legitimate material of his dance.

Patiently, with proper documentation, numbers of problems will be resolved. Gone will be the feeling of inadequacy and indecision, lessened will be the danger of triviality. The spurious emotion of an older method will give way to authentic emotional concomitants of the substantial meanings. The preliminary study will culminate in logical organizations of material which may suggest form. Technique can derive from the subject matter quite directly, and all the visual and auditory accompaniments of the dance will spring from the same source, near integration from the beginning.

Sounds Utopian? Think of the hard work for a moment and the glow will fade. It will be hard work for a student to develop a whole matrix of fact out of which a fancy in full-bloom may rise, and harder still for the dance instructor to persuade the dancer to embrace such an assignment whole heartedly. But composition is difficult—a serious and responsible kind of work. And it is seriously, wonderfully, worth any trouble.

AMERICAN INDIAN DANCE

The prime consideration in this article shall be the dances of the plains and Southwestern Indians. However, we must recognize the geographical areas of the country and the importance they play upon the cultures of the various tribes. We may freely divide the areas into the Eastern Woodland tribes and the tribes of the Plains, the people of the Southwest and the peoples of the Western Coastal Sections. In each area, a cultural pattern arose due to the environment. The Eastern Woodland tribes were principally sedentary, living in large villages, with an agricultural and slave economy. The Indians of the Plains were nomadic, depending upon the migrations of the buffalo. The Indians of the Southwest were both sedentary and nomadic. (The peoples following a sedentary existence in some cases built their villages on mesas to protect themselves from the maurading nomads.) The peoples of the Western Coast lived in villages, practiced slavery and depended, to a great extent, upon fishing for a livelihood.

In each section a very different and elaborate pantheon arose. There is a similarity in each area, as regards dress, design, personal ornament, and dances. The two exceptions to this are the marked differences in language and music.

The Indians of the Plains and Southwest can give present available materials for study, whereas the Eastern groups have been eradicated or forced to disperse and move west, leaving no records.

Some of the Eastern Plains tribes such as the Mandans, Hidatas and Omahas live in villages with houses made of logs, sod and brush. The tipi, or conical tent, used farther west was

Lester Horton, *Educational Dance*, Vol. 4, No. 4 (October) 1941.

made of buffalo hides, easily struck and erected at the command of the police or "council." Transportation was by the dog (the only beast of burden until the coming of the horse), and transportation followed the buffalo, the main staple food.

It is not curious, then, that in this section dances should develop around the hunt, nor is it curious that in the Southwest dances developed as a prayer for rain and growth. Also on the plains dances originated to develop or instill courage and valor, as in the Sun Dance and the Scalp Dance.

The dances of the plains may be divided into these groups: Personal Totem Dance (sacred), Dances of the Secret Societies (sacred and social), Hunting Dances, Pleasure Dances, and Scalp Dances (a society may govern any of these), and Medicine Dances.

When a boy reached a certain age (usually at puberty) he was advised to go to a lonely spot and fast. After a designated time he returned and spoke only to the "medicine man" and related his dreams. If an object appeared in his vision, such as an animal, stone, etc., this object would become his personal totem. If a particle of this object were obtainable, he carried it in a pouch with his umbilical cord and it became his protector. He made a song about it and often danced to it, about it or for it, depending upon the occasion. His intentions or the words of the song were never made public.

Each tribe was divided into clans (families) and the clans would have societies for men, for women, and for both. Aside from the family societies, other societies were in existence—religious groups, police and governing bodies. Each society had specific dances, both religious and social. The structure of the societies is so complex and varied in each tribe that it will not serve our purpose more than to mention them as a very important factor in tribal life.

Hunting dances centered around the buffalo. When the communal larders were empty, elaborate ceremonies were performed mimicking the buffalo. After a successful hunt a dance of praise was given.

Scalp dances were victory dances and usually permitted each participant in a foray to recount his adventures. Victory dances were never performed before a battle, as there was seldom time, although the women would sing songs and dance for the victory of the men who were away. On the return of the war party, the names of the missing would be told and the immediate ceremony would be a combination of victory and dirge. These ceremonies were often called "singing of the scalps." The scalps secured were hung from a long pole and paraded through the village. During the dance each participant recounted his deeds, which had to be verified by witnesses. He was permitted a certain ornament for his valor. Out of these collections grew the war bonnet and the feather bustle.

Shaman dances were performed by "Medicine Men" for all kinds of illnesses. The character of the dance and the songs were the sole property of the doctor and the ailment treated had a specific formula. Powerful medicine songs, totem songs and dances might be bought. In recent years and since the laying down of tribal wars, special songs and dances have been purchased. The Hoop dance is an example. Originating among the Sioux, it now appears among many tribes of Indians and has become the most popular of the exhibition dances in Taos.

The dances of the Plains are characterized by a looseness of structure which permits a license in personal improvisation. In marked contrast are the highly organized group dances of the Pueblos, almost without exception uniformly costumed and rehearsed before being performed. The Pueblo dances are characterized by set choreographic patterns, usually symmetrical, traveling in circles, lines, wedges and "checkerboard" with very marked asymmetrical steps.

A common characteristic among all Indians is a looseness in the knees when executing steps. Most of the steps have a carressing quality and touch the ground with a quick rebound. Exceptions to this are in the side glidings and rotations on the heel.

The dances of the Pueblos are governed by the societies, in many instances. Most of them are concerned with rain, growth and fertility rites. The Snake dance is a prayer for rain; the Eagle dance, a remnant of an ancient rain and growth ceremony. The Rainbow dance of the Eastern Pueblos is likewise a rain ceremony. The Hopi villages and Zuni have an elaborate pantheon with many spirits called *Hacinas*. These figures are elaborately portrayed by masked dancers.

The Navajos living in the same territory as the Pueblos have an equally interesting array of "gods" to which they dance. If the rites are not as elaborately contrived as the Pueblos', we find an adherence to set rituals, prescribed steps and chants for all occasions. The personal decorative motif seems to be transposed to the sacred sand paintings in most of the dance rituals. As in the Pueblo ceremonies, corn pollen and the maize head appear as prime symbols. The Navajos and their neighbors, the Apaches, were marauding nomads until the Spaniards introduced the horse, sheep, and goat. These, with the introduction of silver, modified the culture of the Navajo, who became somewhat sedentary. Wherever the horse came into use dances and songs originated about the animal.

Personal and group adornment in costume and masks reached a high point in three areas of primitive society: among the Pueblo peoples, the Indians of the Northwest, and the Slave Coast of Africa. The masks of the Pueblos differ from the others due to the immediate materials of construction. Large pieces of wood were not available and the Pueblo artist constructed masks from parfleche or rawhide, and built them up often on large constructions and extensions. One of the most arresting pieces of ornament is the tablet headdress worn by the women in various dances. It is beautiful in effect and symbol. Often the bangs of the women hang over the eyes as half masks. The masks of the Apache "Devil" dancers recall a similar construction in Africa. They are made of leather or cloth fitting over the head tightly with slits for eyes. To these are attached constructions extending out and upward made of yucca tythes [sic]. They demonstrate a very remarkable design basis and are usually painted black and white.

The steps listed may be used for classroom work in any grade level. Most of the steps fall into a 2/4 pattern, but may be experimented with in various meters. Dropping of eighth notes will give a syncopation series. The steps may be combined in various patterns and combinations, regardless of the tribe or type of step.

Characteristic Dance Steps of the Plains Indians

1. Toe Heel. Step on ball of foot, lower heel as other foot comes forward. Executed with loose knees.

2. Toe Heel Fast. Same as No. 1, but is executed much faster, which tends to keep the feet forward and from under the body.

3. Toe Heel Tap. Tap toe forward, raise toe and pull foot back, lower heel as other foot comes forward. This gives a placement which may be counted toe, toe, heel, and the last toe-heel is equivalent to one-eighth note. The body has an upright and forward spring on the first tap. This step is executed very rapidly and the feet seem to be always off the earth. There is a distinct rotary action back, up and over in the movement. The Comanche step of the Pueblo Indians is almost identical.

4. Toe Heel Across. Step same as in No. 1, but the leading foot crosses over the back.

5. Toe Heel Spread. It is customary among the Shoshoni men to execute the toe heel in a deep squat position. The feet are turned out and the body sways laterally away from the leading foot.

6. Kutenai Toe Heel. The feet are spread as in the Shoshoni step and turned outward. Before the toe is put down there is a high, springing movement of the knee. The heel hits

lightly, the body pushes away from the leading leg. There is a continual vibration in the body.

7. Osage Toe Heel. The leading foot crosses extremely over the back foot and the toe is placed down, dragged back as the heel descends. This action cuts the back foot out, which is brought forward and repeated. The step does not allow for rapid progression. The effect is of a strut and is usually accompanied by a shaking of the complete musculature.

8. Blackfoot Point. Strike the point of the toe forward; as the foot recovers flat, the other toe strikes forward. Executed very rapidly and lightly.

9. Side Step. Step to side, foot forward, draw other foot to it. Repeat. Short and rapid with knees very loose.

10. Side Step Heel. Step sideways on heel. Twist on heel, letting the ball or toe point to drawing foot, which drags to a closed position. At the conclusion of one step the leading foot should be pigeon-toed in and the other straight forward. This is a characteristic women's step and is performed in a circle.

Characteristic Steps of the Southwestern Indians

1. Women's Step from the Buffalo Dance. Stand with feet close together, knees flexed. Move toes to R., follow with heels. Repeat rapidly, keeping feet together. This step is performed in a straight line of direction. It may extend longer to one direction.

2. High Trot of the Buffalo Dance. The two buffaloes execute a high trot step as a means of locomotion. The knees are brought high without destroying the verticality of the

spine. The arms move downward in opposition to the legs. This is a characteristic step of the Pueblos.

3.   High Trot Double. Performed on the balls of the feet. The knee is brought high and as the foot descends there is a double bounce, bringing the foot slightly forward. This is a "dust-making" step. A characteristic of all Pueblo dances is the held beat coming at different intervals either down or up (off the ground).

4.   Eagle Dance Step. Tap the R. toe obliquely forward or side drag the other foot. This step is executed very rapidly and at different time lengths. The body arm [sic] is raised without destroying the straight line of the wings.

5.   Eagle Shuffle. Another characteristic step is the rapid shuffle. The knee is brought high and as the leg descends the foot scrapes forward similar to the action of running a thumb over a tambourine. The legs rotate back, down and forward.

6.   Eagle Pivot. The Eastern Pueblos use a pivot step in the Eagle Dance. The body weight leans away from the pulsing leg. Hop on 1 count and push the leg away from the supporting leg and tap the toe four times in a half circle. The supporting foot twists or hops to execute the circle. Full circles may be used as a means of locomotion by making half circles. Various counts are used and the circle always moves front.

7.   "Kachna Step." A characteristic step from the large group dances. Lift the R. knee high and simultaneously drop or limp the left foot forward. Repeat. The Rattle accompanies the R. leg. The characteristic halt is used at different intervals, often with a double beat down with the leading leg. The halt may be a signal to change leading legs. This is a characteristic step of the Navajo "Mountain Chant."

The supporting leg is loose and the step does not travel rapidly.

8. Jump Steps.
    A. Jump forward on L. foot. Jump forward on R.
    B. Jump forward on both feet. Jump forward on R. and raise L. sharply forward and up. Repeat or alternate.
    C. Repeat B, pulling the free leg from the rear.
    D. Jump forward on L. foot. Hop on L. foot and raise R. to back. Hop back on R. Hop on R. and bring L. forward. Repeat.

9. Hop Step with Heel Stroke. Hop on R. foot. Strike L. heel on ground rear and foot line forward. Hop on L. foot and raise R. leg back sharply. Repeat.

10. Hop Side. Hop gently to R. on R. foot and tap L. heel at R. heel and tap L. heel away from R. Repeat.

The description of the gestures is not possible as they practically defy analysis. But many of the dances have a symbol gesture understood collectively by the people. For example, the Corn dance, a limp hand palm down denotes rain; and the palm up with two fingers extended symbolizes the sprouting corn. The line of the body, the action of the head, the manner in which the rattle is used, all have a meaning.

NEW DANCE EXPLAINED AS EVOLUTION

Present-Day Artist, Designer Shows, Goes on From Past
By Isabel Morse Jones

The modern dance and modern dancers have been under
admiring and also acrimonious discussion several seasons.

At long last, lecture-demonstrations in Los Angeles will
make a laudable attempt at explanation. Lester Horton, a leader
among contemporary dance designers, allowed us to look over
his shoulder and into his notebook. His talk with the Horton
Concert Group Studio was enlivened with impressive examples
from the dancers.

Term Insufficient

"We all agree that the term modern dance is insufficient. Its
name implies that it is ever present and contemporary, which it
is. It was born of the desire to create a vital, contemporary art
form.

"The classic dance created an elaborate system embellished
by masters during several hundred years. It became an art of
virtuosity. A performer was noted for his technique. The idea
was secondary.

"The modern dancer as well as the modern painter, sculptor
and musician, is cognizant of the past but wishes to go forward.
There is much to learn about movement. The modern schools
are all concerned with techniques but not at the sacrifice of
content or something to say.

Quotations from a Horton Lecture Demonstration. From an article by
Isabel Morse Jones in the *Los Angeles Times,* February 20, 1939.

Only in Choreo-Drama

"The modern dancer does not intend to act except in a choreo-drama. Even then he does not suggest improvisation but times each phrase according to the choreographic design. This one development may usher in a new technique of theater dance.

"The principal achievement of the new dance is the projecting of vital ideas through bodily movement, by distortion, stress and accent, relation to space, changes of intensity and so on.

"The critic has a difficult time describing a dance—at most he can praise or condemn what has been accomplished.

Summarizes Situation

"Often there is a narrative, most often not. In the latter case the performer summarizes a situation or a state of mind. This procedure is called abstraction in the modern dance.

"The new dance appeals to the younger generation. Youngsters see nothing strange in the movement which often shocks and dismays their elders. Many of the colleges are teaching the modern dance and for the first time men are interested.

"Any departure from the normal is distortion. The modern dance is no more distorted than the classic. Rising to the points and executing forty fouettés is just as distorted as hip-swing falls and shoulder jerks.

Human Limitations

"The human body is limited and the distortions of body planes cannot be compared to the arts of painting and sculpture. We confuse our terminology."

program notes

RITE OF SPRING (LE SACRE DU PRINTEMPS)

1. Tribal Response to Spring

The Primitive agriculturists were inactive during the winter and they eagerly awaited the first signs of spring which were greeted with rejoicing and with a period of great activity and expectation for good planting; and prayers for the fertility of nature.

2. Dance of the Adolescents

In the spring, too, primitive tribes held ceremonials teaching those who had come of age the laws and customs of the tribe. They were put through long and difficult tests, and those who were successful in passing these tests became full-fledged members of the tribe if boys, and if girls, they were declared ready for marriage.

3. Ritual of Spring Mating

Spring was the period of mating. Wooing of young maidens was a highly formalized procedure, often culminating in a ritual of Mock Abduction.

August 5, 1937. Hollywood Bowl.

215

4.   Vernal Dance

The celebration of tribal marriages was a community affair, performed as a kind of Spring Round Dance. The most sacred ritual symbol of the primitive was the circle. It represented the sun, moon, passage of the seasons; was a secure protection from outside enemies, and their most sacred rites were always danced in a circle. This early belief and symbol has carried down through the ages to modern Folk Dances and our own wedding rings.

5.   Tribal War Games

Primitive war was entirely confined to personal combat, and training for it consisted of dancing; going through the action of thrusting, feinting, etc. The most famous historical war dances were the Pyrrhic dances of Greece. In war dances the entire tribe took part, the men dancing and exhibiting their prowess, while the women and children encouraged them to the proper pitch of fury and bravery.

6.   Procession of the Sage

Every tribe had a Sage, and it was his duty to completely memorize and lead the others in all intricate rituals. In Mr. Horton's conception of this ballet he has designed his choreography so that into the excited dance of war and personal exhibitionism, the Sage or Wise Man of the tribe comes to begin the ritual of Spring Planting, and prayers for fertility. He performs a dance of Mystery, based upon the sacred Magic Circle.

7.   Adoration of the Earth

Worked into a religious ecstacy by the gyrations of the Sage, the entire tribe joins in a dance of Magic, in supplication to the good spirits of the earth, stamping on the earth to waken it from its winter sleep, leaps to denote how high the grain should grow. Grotesque, frantic dances to frighten away the evil spirits of barren ground and sterile seed.

8. Mystery of the Magic Circles

All tribes at this time of year offered some sacrifice to the earth spirits. Many of these were "Blood" sacrifices, for they thought to pour blood upon the ground replenished it and gave it new life and so assured good crops. There were as many ways of making this sacrifice as there were tribes but, with little exception, if the sacrifice was to be a human offering, the choosing was made by the Sage of the tribe who went into a trance to make sure of a choice which would please the earth spirits. In this ballet the sacred rite of choosing employs the Magic Circle as the design of the dance. Weaving in circles, creating the spell which will aid the Sage in his choice of a virgin for sacrifice.

9. Glorification of the Chosen One

When the Sage finally made his choice, the tribes would deify the purity and holiness of the One chosen for this great religious sacrifice, she who lays down her life that the rest of the tribe may have good crops and live.

10. Ritual of Ancestor Worship

Ancestor Worship was always of great importance and spiritual significance to the primitives, and was performed at both Spring and Fall festivals. Ancestor Worship rituals were exclusively a male form of worship for it was the male ancestor who was worshipped, and women were not considered high enough or sufficiently holy to take part in this dance of deep religious ecstasy.

11. Sacrificial Dance of Chosen One

Having been bathed and anointed, bedecked in symbolic sacrificial robes, the Chosen One, a human who has been made so Holy that although she is a woman she receives the adoration accorded male ancestors, is brought forth for the ceremony.

She starts her dance of sacrifice, trancelike, as the tribe members watch her, fascinated. As she dances more wildly, in greater ecstasy, the hypnotic spell manifests itself in her watchers by spontaneous movements of prayer and supplication, as she finally dances herself to death.

TIERRA Y LIBERTAD!

Tierra Y Libertad

An epic ballet in five episodes, wherein characters and figures symbolize forces and masses of people. Choreography by Lester Horton. Music by Adrian MacDermott. Scripts by Steve Pratt. Costumes and scenery by Guadalupe Martinez. Music directors, Adrian MacDermott, Miriam Brooks. Narration, Victor Heyden.

Prologo-Leyenda

Jim Mitchell as Quetzalcoatl, Herman Bodendorfer as Tezcatlipoca.

A ceremonial dance ushers in the God Quetzalcoatl, the great teacher. The Indians perform a pastoral-like dance of gratitude. Tezcatlipoca and two necromancers interrupt and persuade the God to partake of a new beverage. The effect is immediate to the delight of the rivals, and to the horror of the people, pulled into a compulsive drunken dance. In anger and humiliation, Quetzalcoatl leaves his people, leaving his mask behind as a token to be reclaimed in the hour of his return.

Conquista

Three figures of the conquest—Herman Bodendorfer as the Crown, Leon Rapoport as the State, Eleanor Brooks as the Church. Jeri Faubion and Bella Lewitzky as Indians.

The Indians, believing the figures to be the descendents of Quetzalcoatl, present the mask in reverence. They are set upon, forced into bondage, and the mask destroyed.

This work premiered on Nov. 3, 1939. A later version appears in the Program Notes.

Inquisicion

Eleanor Brooks as the figure of the inquisition and later the
ecclesiastical judge. Jeri Faubion as the Heretic. Bella Lewitzky
as the Indian.

The heretic and Indian are brought before the court. The
execution of the heretic on the rack does not cow the Indian
into submission. The garrote is the reward.

Mestizaje

Eleanor Brooks as the figure, a triune symbol. Bella Lewitzky as
the figure of revolt.

The Indians are forced into strange cultural patterns. Some dare
to raise the cry of the Aztecs, "The land belongs to him who
tills it."

Celebracion

Bella Lewitzky as the prophetic figure.

Call is a signal for celebration. The celebration of freedom, the
celebration of independence and agrarian reforms. The
celebration of heroes, Padre Hidalgo, Benito Juarez and Emiliano
Zapata.

SOMETHING TO PLEASE EVERYBODY

[Spoken] Commentary

I.   Opening

Good evening, ladies and gentlemen, this is ----------------------, your program notes by proxy, introducing "SOMETHING TO PLEASE EVERYBODY," a concert revue. We present, for your pleasure, the artists for the evening: --------JERI, DAVID, JIM, ELEANOR, MAXINE, HERMAN, LEON, MAE, BELLA.---------

II.   Murder Mystery

The devotees of "Whodunit" may enjoy the bad, bad Manners family, and what transpired when they read the strange last will and testament of elderly, and eccentric Josiah Manners.--------

I, Josiah Manners, do bequeath my sole wordly possessions, to be allotted according to details as herein given. The recipient of my fortune shall be selected at random from one of six sealed envelopes, to be given one to each of my expectant heirs. In the event of fatal mishap to the first chosen, the second heir must be determined in a similar manner. In the event of the sudden demise of the second heir, and also of further rightful heirs, the same procedure must be followed. I hereby swear that I am this day in sound mind and body, and the above details are in accordance with my own will.

Sworn before me this day of our Lord.

signed—Josiah Manners.
executor—Winthrop Stebbins.

November 3, 1939. Philharmonic Auditorium.

III. Romance

The tender and lyric values inherent in the romantic theme——
colored with the overtones of nostalgia and the threat of parting.

IV. Dithyrambos

Today we possess but little factual information concerning the
classic Grecian dance, although certain names have come down to
us with some vague meanings implied. Dithyrambos, in an exultant
and heroic vein, is a hymn of praise and ceremonial intoxication to
Bacchus, god of festival, the grape, and the wine press.

V. Carib

The negroes and people of mixed blood of Haiti, Cuba, and Santo
Domingo have compounded a dance out of French, Spanish, and
African materials which is as fresh as the primitive and as full of
suggestion as the most sophisticated duet. ——Half cock-fight, and
half love-making.

VI. Madrigal Doloroso

The smoldering dances of Spain reflect a somber history, the
story of the life of a people obstructed by brutal defeat on the
road to freedom. Since 1936, Spain's sorrow is the shame and
burden of all the western world.

VII. Sordid Sweetmeats

The theater is full of erotic patterns. Some are low and bawdy,
some are robust and wholesome. Some of them are in the great
tradition and have a high intellectual sanction.

VIII.   Tragedy

The indomitable courage and resistance shown by the Chinese peasant in the face of overwhelming military superiority is a source of pride for all the free peoples of the earth. We may especially remember their patient stoicism during the merciless bombing of Chung-King, when they fled to their fields for protection and found only straw.

IX.   Primitive

The appeal of the primitive is enduring and wide. Its simple statements have an air of the fundamental. The pulsation of its insistent rhythm is heard as the men perform.

X.   Nautch

The oriental forms have long been favorites among dance enthusiasts. We present Nautch, a composite of many styles, all Eastern in origin.

XI.   Surrealism

A great number of new aesthetic forms have crawled forth into the bright light of day in a comparatively few years. ——Cubism, and after came Dadaism, and after Dada, Surrealism unveiled its rotting flesh on lurid bones. It is an age of penitential hair tea cups; bandages and crutches have come into their own; and locomotives may be made of lace.

XII.   Hoop Dance

All primitive peoples have certain dances of a purely entertainment value. Most of these are of a distinctly spectacular nature with an accent on technical virtuosity. This Hoop dance is taken from the athletic dance of the Pueblo Indians.

XIII.   Boogie-Bali-Woogie

The dance of Bali and Java, dug, hep, and jived up to the tempo of our own "but zoot," Boogie Woogie. We give you now—The Java Jig, or, Eight beat à la Balinese.

XIV.   Finale

Ladies and gentlemen, once in the life of every revue, comes the finale, with the traditional and time-honored medley. Our offering is chosen from Nautch, Primitive, Surrealism, Sordid Sweetmeats, and Boogie Bali Woogie. ——Hoping that our work has truly been,—— "SOMETHING TO PLEASE EVERYBODY."——

scenarios

BARREL HOUSE

Scene

The working area is framed by a series of white, transparent screens. They are lighted from behind. In the center-back area is a square piano—preferably black. A white horse's jaw rests on the panel board at the player's left. The piano is flanked on the right by a low black bench.

The performers are on stage thru-out. No exits or entrances are made. The beginning positions: The Dancer-Player is seated at the piano. Standing at his right is another male dancer. A third is seated at the bench audience endwards (he plays clappers thru various parts). The girl is center right.

The work is divided into three main sections and may be called "Plaint" (or "Bordello Sob"), "Gut Bucket," and "Gully Low." All are a synthesis of blues. The third section develops into a violent protest.

Action

Music prelude before curtain. The Dancer-Player is discovered with his head tilted backwards. The dancer at his right performs a monotonous rhythmic action thru-out the first section. The

December 13, 1947. Philharmonic Auditorium. Words in italics were spoken aloud.

225

seated dancer has no movement during the first section. The dance of the girl is projected as a series of very personal plaints.

A.   Interrogation—*What is the end?*

The Dancer-Player's only action aside from the compensations of fingering is the head-up-and-back attitude with occasionally poignant dropping accents of his head to his chest. His theme develops with the action of the girl—and small head circles come into play near the end of the first sequence. The dancer to his right continues one action thru-out the first part.

B.   Day Past-Gone

C.   Men's Hands

D.   Bitter Misery

Music note: Dropped measures are characteristic during this part.

Transition

The girl's action moves her on to the bench where the last part is performed. At the end she falls on the dancer standing at the piano, and ends with the horse's jaw in her hand. This motivates the second part. The second part has a simple accompaniment— piano (one hand), the horse's jaw and clappers.

Gut-Bucket

(The Dancer-Player)

A.   Interrogation—*What is the end?*

B.   *Want freedom before I die.*

C.   Rebuke—*Freedom has a price.*

D.   Interrogation—*What is the end?*

Transition

Part D motivates the dancer on the bench and the dancer playing the jaw. The girl takes the jaw and the only accompaniment is the jaw, breath, noises, finger and foot beats. During the transition the Dancer-Player resumes his place at the piano, the condition of which does not prevent him from dancing during the third section.

Gully Low

A. *Moan our troubles together.*
    Girl and Dancer on the bench

B. *Want freedom before I die.*
    Trio

C. *Freedom has a price.*

BROWN COUNTY, INDIANA

Action Area

At center stage rear is an upright post describing one corner of a
house. Running from the upright to stage right rear is described
a section of the house which has a doorway. From the center
upright to stage left rear is described the other side of the house.
Where both sides end at back curtain, the design is continued
onto the back drop as a log cabin, and the hills of Brown
County are also juxtaposed in the design. The frame-work must
be slim to reveal the action within the house. Items of furniture
will be added as needed in the choreographic plan. Props must
be kept to the minimum although their usage is a challenge in
modern dance. Noticeable is a sickle stuck in the up-stage side of
the doorway. A long box is placed in the front corner of the
house.

Dancers

A Quaker Widow
Her Daughter
An Escaping Slave
Her Pursuer

Action

1. The widow in the doorway carries Bible. Her daughter is by
    her side. Morning prayers. They retire to interior. Widow
    places the Bible on the black box.

July, 1950. Dance Theater. This is a first draft. The final version differed in
a number of details.

2. Daughter takes bucket and dipper, pauses in doorway for a momentary praise of the earth and its goodness, exits.

3. The widow stops in door in kindred action of daughter. She moves forward to front stage and looks to rear spanning her homesite. She rolls up sleeves, enters house and puts on apron.

4. The daughter enters as mother comes through doorway. Daughter takes an early summer apple from her apron and tosses it to her mother. The mother praises the apple and places it on the window sill. The daughter waits in doorway as—

5. Mother takes the sickle and departs. The daughter places the bucket in the rear of the room. She dances in synthesis of chores.

6. The slave enters from stage right. She is near exhaustion. She turns and runs, slips back again hoping to meet protective friends.

7. The daughter comes to door. The girl hugs house side and vanishes out of sight. The daughter looks out doorway and comes outside of house opposite to the girl's side in action of chore.

8. The girl reappears, sees apple. Famished, she seizes it. The daughter appears. The girl runs, drops apple. The daughter grabs apple, pursues the girl, holds the apple towards her. The girl, hungry but distrustful comes for it.

9. The girl takes the apple and collapses. The daughter attempts to revive her. She pulls her into the chair.

10. The widow appears with shock of wheat and the sickle. She sees the girl in the chair. She circles stage looking offstage for any sign of pursuers. In anger she impales the sickle in its former place and drops the wheat under the window.

11.   They take the girl into the house. She revives and struggles hysterically and runs outside, circles stage to return to them.

12.   The pursuer enters from stage right. The girl stiffens. The daughter runs to window, falls back. They hide the girl in the box.

13.   The daughter comes to door, deliberately comes out and picks up chair, places it in doorway. Sits in it and rocks. Mother performs pattern of indifference. The pursuer stalks across and around stage (as animal trainer).

14.   He moves to doorway. The girl does not give. He moves away, returns, cracks his whip. The daughter stands, is joined by mother.

15.   He demands entry. The mother forces arm across doorway.

16.   He forces the arm down with the butt of his whip. The daughter flings herself at him, knocking him backwards. He retaliates by lashing at the widow and daughter.

17.   He forces entry. Looks for girl. Finds her in box. She comes out. He menaces her.

18.   She runs from house, he pursues—cracks his whip. She stops. The widow and daughter beseech him for mercy.

19.   He whips the girl. The widow in righteous anger grabs the whip from him—flails him. He recoils. His arrogance gone, he is frightened. She lashes him, he falls backward over box—stunned.

talking about horton

RUDI GERNREICH

Lester had a genius for drawing people out of themselves . . .
finding out what their talents were. The great thing about him
was his openness— He had no formulas and no limitations. He
seemed always to be asking, 'What are the possibilities?' My
work with him gave me a special awareness and understanding of
the way clothes behave on a figure in motion. His sense of
plastic form was incredible. I learned so much from him—things
that still influence my work now.

Excerpt from interview with author, August 25, 1970, Los Angeles.

LOU HARRISON

14 · 111 · '68   Aptos

DEAR MARRY ARREN

Thanx for your letter & question. ¢ Bill
Bowne gave me a copy of Dance Persp²,
which I nostalgically read cover to cover.
I was much influenced by Lester, his magic
stimulus, imagination, humor & general
loveliness. Certainly he was much ahead
(present theater developements are closer
to him than ever) & working with him
was always exciting.
Years before knowing Lester I was already
full of admiration for the great artists

of Mexico (who, in the thirties, could not have been??) &, too, of the composers Carlos Chavez & (by reputation) Revueltas. Chavez's music was early published in New Music Edition, & Henry Cowell even acquainted me with the music to Chavez's ballet " H.P.", by means of old aluminum dubbing discs.

But it was Lester who "full-scale" alerted me to the glories of Mexico as "folk-culture" & "classical-ancient culture". Through his own singing I first heard La Sandunga & many other such melodies. (I suddenly realize that this aspect of Lester is right now identically alive in the Ballet Folklorico's work.— tho perhaps Lester's were the finer choreographies) I learned the basic outline of Mexican history from him, & continue to this day to fill it in.

I always felt completely "in tune" working with

2

Lester. There was the wonderful matter of working with another male (an infrequent chance for a young musician-among dancers in those days), &, in addition to the sensation of intimate love & support general in the whole group, there was always that fabulous fantasy - playfullness - theatric delight. My own feel for the theater seemed perfectly to mesh with his - I think that this has never happened fully to me since - the concern with all aspects of it. As I had pre-adolescently fallen in love with Yeats "Four Plays for Dancers", the masks & the music of Dulac & of George Anthiel, it was only natural to find myself "costuming" & "setting" with Lester when we 1st did a large work together. Maybe due to his own driving intensity I have never lost my pleasure in doing all sorts of things other than the music for which I am known. Anyway, it always has seemed real

3

to me that Lester's-type — the type of the full
artist — should "create all over the place" — have
a ball — PLAY !
When we are children we go about our play very
seriously & absorbedly indeed — we do this
because, of course, it isn't play unless it is
serious & absorbing. When we are "grown up"
we do the same thing — we play — & we
then call it Civilization.
Lester never forgot that for a moment !

Please keep me in touch with what you
do, & about that magic & marvelous
man !
                              Best wishes from
                              Lou Harrison

CONSTANTINE HASSALEVRIS

In the early 1950s as the Hollywood Correspondent for *Dance News* I did a review of a program at Dance Theater which was generally complimentary, but in the last paragraph there were some negative comments. To my surprise, I found that Lester had posted the review in its entirety in the showcase in front of the theater as part of the display. When I suggested that he cut off the last few sentences, he just smiled at me. He wouldn't consider it.

Lester, in his last years, hated doing some of the commercial work. He said the only thing that kept him from feeling like a whore was that his material was better than the average work of that kind. That was as bragging a statement as I ever heard him make. The money of course was always pumped back into the theater. He had enjoyed the work earlier in his life but toward the end was, I think, angry that he hadn't been successful enough so that he didn't have to take these jobs. He didn't give a damn about money, but he had to survive and his theater had to survive.

In those days I specialized in dance photography and remember sessions with his company. Before the sitting he would show them how to do proper make-up for studio photography, which is different from stage make-up. The poses would be preplanned, and much more could be accomplished because of the work he had done in advance. The dancers were learning professionalism of the first order. He was a perfectionist without that obnoxious ego that goes with it.

Now they are trying to deify him. It is unfair to his memory. He would have hated it. He was a man like any man doing his work as well as he could.

Excerpt from interview with author, August 15, 1970, Los Angeles.

JAMES TRUITTE

My first impression of Horton was of a stocky man, about 5'10" with a compassionate face and penetrating eyes . . . the very beautiful crop of grey hair. The greeting I got when I first registered at the school told me that this was where I should be. He had that kind of warmth. Anyone who met him once remembered him. He was kind of electric. He had unconventional taste in clothing. He could wear an orange silk shirt with a pale pink tie [this was in the early 1950s]. Then he might wear a red shirt with a green tie. On him it looked good. We all learned from that. We learned how colors could blend by watching him tie-dye.

He never told us how to teach, but he would drop bombshells in conversations: 'You don't play favorites. If there are twenty-five people in the class then you have to talk to twenty-five people at the same time. In that hour and a half you have to make each of these people aware that you are their teacher.' Occasionally you could sense someone out there in the theater and you knew it was Lester. He'd watch for ten minutes or so and then disappear into the costume room. Any comments on teaching would come out later, at another time, in conversation.

He wouldn't sit down and give you these great explanations with imageries. You'd get it mostly just by working. If you happened to ask him something, he'd say, 'I'll think about it, I'll let you know later.' That was his way of saying, probe into your own part, you're doing it, not me. It worked very well.

In class he stressed performing techniques, phrasing, and musicality. I have seen him stop people in class and ask them,

Excerpt from interview with author, June 3, 1973, New York City.

'Who are you? If you're you, don't try to dance like him or her. Dance like yourself.' He told us, 'Your own personal individuality is your most priceless asset. When I want seventeen dancers on the stage, I want seventeen personalities.' Lester didn't want to make little Lester Hortons out of us.

Lester challenged each one of us to do something other than what we were all capable of doing well. Sometimes he went so far as to have us do parts which were not exactly right for us, just for the experience. He made me do "Dedication to Orozco" which was difficult for my body. The fight I put up! But the experience has worn me well. That was part of his genius.

et cetera

HORTON'S EASY BORSCH

He started with a big can of tomatoes and a big can of diced beets, which he put together in a large pot. Then he made very small meat balls with onions and garlic—floured them and browned them in a skillet. When they were cooked, he added them to the beets and tomatoes and cooked them together for a while and then served the whole thing in Persian bowls with a dollop of sour cream. Together with hot, buttered French bread and salad, it was an unforgettable meal.

Recipe courtesy of Elizabeth Talbot-Martin.

DANCE THEATER CONTRACT [1953]

Repertory Dance Company Agreement

In the group interests and for the purpose of securing work for the group as a unit, the following has been set up as a legal and binding contract between Dance Theater and members of the Dance Theater Repertory Company, to wit:

I, _____, a member of the Dance Theater Repertory Company, hereby commit myself to a twelve (12) month contract with Dance Theater, whereby in exchange for my training and the opportunities presented therein I agree to the following conditions.

1:   I will work with and dance with the Dance Theater Repertory Company in all capacities as directed by Dance Theater and/or Lester Horton.

2:   I will accept no outside work that interferes with performances at Dance Theater, 7566 Melrose Avenue, Los Angeles 46, California; and I will furthermore accept no outside work that materially interferes with rehearsals and training for these performances, unless approved by Dance Theater.

3:   I will be available for all rehearsal calls reasonably set in advance.

4:   I agree to the inclusion of my name and fully accept the responsibility thereof in any group contract for domestic or overseas engagements at minimum wage scales established by the unions involved, or more, or upon a cooperative basis of sharing the profits after production expenses are met. I furthermore agree to the use of my name and photographs for publicity releases at the discretion of Dance Theater.

5:    There can be no early release from this agreement, excepting by special permission granted by Dance Theater and/or Lester Horton. Periods lost through illness or disability arising from accidents, as certified by letter from an accredited physician, extend this contract automatically for the exact time lost in illness or disability.

The above constitutes a legal and binding agreement entered into by Dance Theater and _____ for a twelve (12) month period starting this _____ day of _____ , 19__ and ending the _____ day of _____, 19__.

_____

by parent or guardian
if under age

_____

Lester Horton for
Dance Theater

chronologies

CHOREOGRAPHIC WORKS OF LESTER HORTON

July 1, 1928. Argus Bowl

> *The Song of Hiawatha*
> Score: various composers. Cast: Donella Donaldson, Lester Horton, and company.

September 2, 1929. Argus Bowl

> *Siva-Siva*
> Score: Sol Cohen. Cast: Katherine Stubergh, Lester Horton.

August 28, 1931. Argus Bowl

> *Kootenai War Dance*
> Score: Percussion. Cast: Lester Horton.

August 8, 1932. Philharmonic Auditorium

> *Voodoo Ceremonial*
> Score: Percussion. Decor: Albert Deano. Cast: Lester Horton, and company.

Unless otherwise specified, all choreographies, scores, decors, and costumes were by Lester Horton. Most of the early percussion scores were arranged by Horton with William Bowne. In these cases, program credit was most frequently given only for choreography. Theaters were all in the Los Angeles area, except those otherwise noted.

September 9, 1932. Little Theater of the Verdugos

Takwish, The Star Maker
Score: Roland Klump. Decor: Jean Abel. Costumes: Jean
Abel, Lester Horton. Cast: Rudolph Abel, Toni Masarachia,
Doje Arbenz, Elizabeth Talbot-Martin, and group.

July 8, 1933. Little Theater of the Verdugos

Oriental Motifs
Score: Percussion. Cast: Lester Horton, and group.

January 19, 1934. Wilshire-Ebell Theater

Allegro Barbaro
Score: Béla Bartók. Cast: Dorothy Wagner, Lester Horton.

May Night
Score: Selim Palmgren. Cast: Dorothy Wagner, Lester
Horton.

February 23, 1934. Little Theater of the Verdugos

Hand Dance
Score: Polynesian (percussion). Cast: Group.

Lament
Score: Hebrew. Cast: Brahm van den Berg.

July 25, 1934. Shrine Auditorium

Incantation from *Aboriginal Suite*
Score: Percussion. Cast: Toni Masarachia.

Dances of the Night
Score: Percussion. Cast: Thelma Leaton, Elizabeth Talbot-
Martin, Joy Montaya.

Two Arabesques
Score: Erik Satie. Cast: Group.

Salome
Score: Constance Boynton. Costumes: Portia Woodbury.
Cast: Joy Montaya, Elizabeth Talbot-Martin, Toni
Masarachia, Brahm van den Berg, Lester Horton, and group.

August 8, 1934. Shrine Auditorium

Aztec Ballet
Score: Percussion (Brahm van den Berg). Decor: Jean Abel.
Costumes: Jean Abel, Lester Horton. Cast: Group.

Second Gnossienne
Score: Erik Satie. Cast: Elizabeth Talbot-Martin.

Concerto Grosso, 2nd Movement
Score: Ernest Bloch. Cast: Thelma Babitz.

Painted Desert Ballet
Score: Homer Grunn. Costumes: Portia Woodbury, Lester
Horton. Cast: Thelma Babitz, Elizabeth Talbot-Martin,
Brahm van den Berg, Bruce Burroughs, Toni Masarachia,
Richard Rogan, Bob Shinn, David Vaughan, and group.

October 26, 1934. Shrine Auditorium

Chinese Fantasy
Score: Percussion. Cast: Elizabeth Talbot-Martin, Brahm
van den Berg, Bruce Burroughs, and group.

November 30, 1934. Philharmonic Auditorium

Bolero
Score: Maurice Ravel. Costumes: Jaron de St. Germain.
Cast: Joy Montaya, Herminia de Ruffo, Brahm van den
Berg, and group.

December 11, 1934. Tuesday Afternoon Club of Glendale

Ave
Score: Zoltán Kodály. Cast: Patty-Max Green.

Maidens
Score: Federico Mompou. Cast: Patty-Max Green, Joewilla Blodgett, Thelma Leaton, Elizabeth Talbot-Martin, and group.

Salutation
Score: Dane Rudhyar. Cast: Lester Horton.

Gnossienne #3
Score: Erik Satie. Cast: Elizabeth Talbot-Martin.

Vale
Score: Zoltán Kodály. Cast: Patty-Max Green.

February 3, 1935. Dance Theater (Norma Gould Studio)

Mound Builders
Score: Sidney Cutner. Costumes: Elizabeth Talbot-Martin and group. Cast: Thelma Leaton, Joy Montaya, Elizabeth Talbot-Martin, Joseph Donavan, Lester Horton, and group.

Antique Suite
Balleto. Score: Simon Molinaro (Arranged by Respighi). Cast: Ana Kurgans. Passacaglia. Score: Ludovico Roncalli (Arranged by Respighi). Cast: Joy Montaya.

Pentecost
Score: Dane Rudhyar. Cast: Lester Horton.

Dictator
Score: Sidney Cutner. Cast: Bruce Burroughs, and group.

Dance of Parting
Score: Vincenzo Davico. Cast: Mary Meyer.

February 22, 1935. Philharmonic Auditorium

Rain Quest
Score: Bertha Miller English. Costumes: Portia Woodbury.
Cast: Elizabeth Talbot-Martin, Renaldo Alarcon, Bruce
Burroughs, Joseph Donavan, Ana Kurgans.

May 24, 1935. Long Beach Masonic Temple

Conflict
Score: Percussion. Cast: Mary Meyer, Lester Horton.

Ritual at Midnight
Score: Constance Boynton. Cast: Joy Montaya, Elizabeth
Talbot-Martin.

Tendresse
Score: Alexander Krien. Cast: Mary Meyer, Lester Horton.

June 25, 1935. Occidental Bowl, Occidental College

Sun Ritual
Score: Bertha Miller English. Cast: Joy Montaya, Renaldo
Alarcon, and group.

July 31, 1935. Brunswig Gardens (private estate)

Rhythmic Dance
Score: Alexandre Tansman. Cast: Mary Meyer.

Salutation to the Depths
Score: Dane Rudhyar. Cast: Elizabeth Talbot-Martin.

December 10, 1935. Figueroa Playhouse

The Mine
Score: Sidney Cutner. Costumes: Elizabeth Talbot-Martin,
Jaron de St. Germain. Cast: Joy Montaya, Lester Horton,
and group.

The Art Patrons
Score: Sidney Cutner. Costumes: Elizabeth Talbot-Martin,
Jaron de St. Germain. Cast: Group.

March 21, 1936. Figueroa Playhouse

Growth of Action
Score: Dane Rudhyar. Cast: Group.

Two Dances for a Leader
Score: Sidney Cutner. Cast: Group.

Flight From Reality
Score: Dane Rudhyar. Cast: Lester Horton.

Lysistrata
Score: Sidney Cutner. Cast: Bella Lewitzky, Mary Meyer,
Ethel Nichols, Clay Dalton, Nathan Kirkpatrick, and group.

July 15, 1936. Hollywood Concert Hall

Ceremony (revision of *Sun Ritual*)
Score: Bertha Miller English. Cast: Bella Lewitzky, Renaldo
Alarcon, Nathan Kirkpatrick, and group.

January 17, 1937. Pasadena Playhouse

Prelude to Militancy
Score: Gian Francesco Malipiero. Cast: Bella Lewitzky.

Chronicle
Score: Sidney Cutner. Cast: Eleanor Brooks, Bella Lewitzky,
Kita van Cleve, Clay Dalton, Nathan Kirkpatrick, and group.

April 26, 1937. Philharmonic Auditorium

Salome (revision)
Score: Bertha Miller English. Cast: Bella Lewitzky, Nathan
Kirkpatrick, Kita van Cleve, Maury Armstrong, Lester Horton.

Prologue to an Earth Celebration
Score: Heitor Villa-Lobos. Art Direction: William Bowne.
Cast: Group.

Exhibition Dance No. I
Score: Bertha Miller English. Art Direction: William Bowne.
Cast: Eleanor Brooks, Bella Lewitzky, Kita van Cleve,
Nathan Kirkpatrick.

August 5, 1937. Hollywood Bowl

Le Sacre du Printemps
Score: Igor Stravinsky. Costumes: William Bowne. Cast:
Bella Lewitzky, Renaldo Alarcon, Brahm van den Berg, and
group.

October 1, 1937. Greek Theater

Salome (revision)
Score: Bertha Miller English. Costumes: Jaron de St.
Germain. Cast: Bella Lewitzky, Kita van Cleve, Renaldo
Alarcon, Lester Horton, Nathan Kirkpatrick.

April 6, 1938. Royce Hall, U.C.L.A.

Pasaremos
Score: Bertha Miller English. Cast: Bella Lewitzky.

Haven
Score: Bertha Miller English. Cast: Charles Pressey and
group.

August 5, 1938. Mills College, Oakland

Conquest
Score: Lou Harrison. Decor: Lou Harrison, Lester Horton.
Costumes: Dorothy Gillanders. Cast: Bella Lewitzky,
Mercier Cunningham, and group.

February 17, 1939. Wilshire-Ebell Theater

Departure From the Land
Score: Gerhardt Dorn. Art Direction: Robert Tyler Lee. Cast:
Eleanor Brooks, Lester Horton, and group.

Five Women
Score: Gerhardt Dorn. Cast: Eleanor Brooks, Eya Fechin,
June Fulton, Kita van Cleve, Pat McGrath.

November 3, 1939. Philharmonic Auditorium

Something to Please Everybody
Score: Lou Harrison. Cast: Group.

Tierra y Libertad! (revision of *Conquest*)
Score: Gerhardt Dorn. Decor & Costumes: William Bowne.
Cast: Eleanor Brooks, Bella Lewitzky, Lester Horton, Brahm
van den Berg, and group.

July 6, 1940. Mills College, Oakland

Sixteen to Twenty-Four
Score: Lou Harrison. Cast: Bella Lewitzky, and group.

November 15, 1940. Wilshire-Ebell Theater

A Noble Comedy (revision of *Lysistrata*)
Score: Simon Abel. Cast: Eleanor Brooks, Bella Lewitzky,
Kita van Cleve, James Mitchell, and group.

May 26, 1941. Assistance League Playhouse

Pavanne
Score: William Byrd. Costumes: Hazel Roy Butler. Cast:
Sonia Shaw.

April 4, 1946. Shubert Theatre, New Haven

Shootin' Star
A Sol Kaplan Musical.

December 13, 1947. Philharmonic Auditorium

Barrel House
Score: Anita Short Metz. Cast: Bella Lewitzky, Herman
Boden, Rudi Gernreich, Carl Ratcliff.

May 22, 1948. Dance Theater

Totem Incantation
Score: Judith Hamilton. Decor & Costumes: William Bowne.
Cast: Constance Finch, Luisa Kreck, Frances Spector, Rudi
Gernreich, Erik Johns, Carl Ratcliff.

The Beloved
Score: Judith Hamilton. Cast: Bella Lewitzky, Herman
Boden.

Salome (revision)
Score: Percussion. Decor: William Bowne. Cast: Bella
Lewitzky, Frances Spector, Herman Boden, Erik Johns,
Rudi Gernreich, Carl Ratcliff.

March 5, 1949. Dance Theater

Warsaw Ghetto
Score: Sol Kaplan. Decor & Costumes: Keith Finch. Cast:
Bella Lewitzky, Sondra Orans.

The Park
Score: Dialogue by Sonia Brown, and street sounds. Decor:
William Bowne. Cast: Luisa Kreck, Bella Lewitzky, Martha
Root, George Allen, Kenneth Bartmess, Rudi Gernreich,
Carl Ratcliff.

The Bench of the Lamb
Score: Mary Hoover. Cast: Constance Finch, and group.

A Touch of Klee and Delightful 2
Score: Camargo Guarnieri. Decor & Costumes: Lewis Brown.
Cast: Constance Finch, Luisa Kreck, Rudi Gernreich, Carl
Ratcliff.

March 21, 1949. Las Palmas Theater

Tongue in Cheek
A musical revue staged by Bella Lewitzky and Lester
Horton.

January 19, 1950. Dance Theater

Estilo De Tù
Score: Aaron Copland, Kenneth Klaus, Milton Rosen.
Decor: Lewis Brown. Costumes: Judith Stander, Lester
Horton. Cast: Luisa Kreck, Bella Lewitzky, Carl Ratcliff,
and group.

A Bouquet For Molly
Score: Earl Robinson. Decor & Costumes: Lewis Brown.
Cast: Bella Lewitzky, Sondra Orans, George Allen, Carl
Ratcliff.

El Rebozo (revision of *The Park*)
Score: Mary Hoover. Decor: William Bowne. Costumes:
George Allen, Lester Horton. Cast: Bella Lewitzky, Luisa
Kreck, Marge Berman, Constance Finch, Kenneth Bartmess,
Rudi Gernreich, Carl Ratcliff.

April 7, 1950. Dance Theater

Salome (revision)
Score: Percussion. Decor: William Bowne. Cast: Carmen de
Lavallade, Luisa Kreck, Sondra Orans, George Allen,
Kenneth Bartmess, Jack Dodds.

July, 1950. Dance Theater

Brown County, Indiana
Score: Kenneth Klaus. Decor: William Bowne. Costumes: Rudi Gernreich. Cast: Luisa Kreck, Carmen de Lavallade, Sondra Orans, Kenneth Bartmess.

Rhythm Section
Score: Percussion. Cast: Company.

March 31, 1951. Dance Theater

Tropic Trio
Score: Audree Covington. Cast: Company.

On the Upbeat
Score: Audree Covington, Milton Rosen. Cast: Company.

Another Touch of Klee
Score: Stan Kenton. Cast: Carmen de Lavallade, Eleanor Johnson, Vida Ann Solomon, Jack Dodds, James Truitte.

May 26, 1951. Ojai Festival

Medea
Score: Audree Covington. Cast: Carmen de Lavallade, Vida Ann Solomon, Renee De Haven, Jack Dodds, James Truitte.

July 21, 1951. Greek Theater

Girl Crazy (revival)
George Gershwin musical.

August 13, 1951. War Memorial Opera House, San Francisco

Annie Get Your Gun (revival)
Irving Berlin musical.

May 23, 1952. Dance Theater

7 Scenes With Ballabilli
Score: Gertrude Rivers Robinson. Costumes: Eleanor
Johnson (under the direction of Lester Horton). Cast: Lelia
Goldoni, Misaye Kawasumi, Joyce Trisler, Norman Cornick,
Henry Dunn, James Truitte.

Liberian Suite
Score: Duke Ellington. Accessories: Martha Koerner. Cast:
Carmen de Lavallade, Richard D'Arcy, James Truitte, and
company.

Prado de Pena
Score: Gertrude Rivers Robinson. Props: Martha Koerner.
Cast: Carmen de Lavallade, Lelia Goldoni, Misaye Kawasumi,
Joyce Trisler, Norman Cornick, Richard D'Arcy, and
company.

March 8, 1953. Wilshire-Ebell Theater

Dedications in Our Time
Score: Gertrude Rivers Robinson. "To Ruth, Mary and
Martha." Cast: Carmen de Lavallade, Sondra Orans, Joyce
Trisler. "Memorial to Hiroshima." Cast: Misaye Kawasumi.
"To Carson McCullers." Cast: Sondra Orans.
Score: Kenneth Klaus. "To José Clemente Orozco." Cast:
Carmen de Lavallade, Jack Dodds. "To Federico Garcia
Lorca." Cast: Carmen de Lavallade, Joyce Trisler, Norman
Cornick, Jack Dodds, James Truitte.

Face of Violence (final version of *Salome*)
Score: Percussion (Lester Horton). Sets & Costumes: Lester
Horton. Cast: Carmen de Lavallade, Joyce Trisler, Misaye
Kawasumi, Norman Cornick, James Truitte.

FILMS CHOREOGRAPHED BY LESTER HORTON

1942   *Moonlight in Havana* (Universal-International)

1943   *Rhythm of the Islands* (Universal-International)
        White Savage (Universal-International)
        Phantom of the Opera (Universal-International)

1944   *Climax* (Universal-International)
        Phantom Lady (Universal-International)
        Ali Baba and the Forty Thieves (Universal-International)
        Gypsy Wildcat (Universal-International)

1945   *Salome, Where She Danced* (Universal-International)
        That Night With You (Universal-International)
        Frisco Sal (Universal-International)
        Shady Lady (Universal-International)

1946   *Tangier* (Universal-International)
        Tarzan and the Leopard Woman (RKO)

1948   *Siren of Atlantis* (United Artists Release)

1949   *Bagdad* (Universal-International)

1952   *Golden Hawk* (Paramount)

1953   *3-D Follies* (RKO)
        South Sea Woman (Warner Brothers)

index

Abel, Jean, 23, 33-35, 38, 194; quoted, 34
African Drum Dance (LH), 105
Ailey, Alvin, 37, 128, 134, 150, 155, 167, 174
Alarcon, Renaldo, 53, 71, 83
Allen, George, 120, 137, 156
American Ballet, The (Shawn), 14
American Dancer, 39, 61, 62, 195; quoted, 29, 54, 64, 66, 84
American Guild of Variety Artists, 103
"American Indian Dance" (article), 204-211
"American Indian Dancing" (excerpt), 29
American in Paris, An (van den Berg), 52
Anderson, Judith, 153
Andre, Juan, 195; quoted, 55
Annie Get Your Gun (LH), 156
Another Touch of Klee (LH), 152, 153
Anthony, Mary, 174
Appalachian Spring (Graham), 80
Arbenz, Doje, 36
"Argus Bowl", 21

Argus, Lysbeth, 21, 22, 29
Arlen, Harold, 107
Armitage, Merle, 80, 92, 94
Armstrong, Maury, 53
Art Patrons (LH), 56
At the Hawk's Well (Yeats), 31
Aztec Ballet (LH), 51, 55

Babitz, Thelma, 51
Bagdad (LH), 136
Bailey, Maurice, 92
Baker, George Pierce, 13, 44
"Bal Caribe" (LH), 157, 188
Barclift, Nelson, 120, 128
Barnes, Clive, 64
Barrel House (LH), 118, 134, 167; (scenario), 225-227
Bartmess, Kenneth, 120, 128, 156
Basis of Modern Dance, The, 156
Bates, Clara Nixon, 12-24 *passim*, 31
Bates, William O., 11, 12, 14, 15, 193; quoted, 13
Beloved, The (LH), 121, 125, 128, 139, 142, 155, 168, 172
Bench of the Lamb (LH), 134, 139
Bennington, Vermont, 106

257

Berman, Marge, 128, 142
Beverly Boulevard studio, 64, 73,
    83, 105, 109
Bird, Bonnie, 86
Black Crook, The, 8
Blodgett, Jeanne, 37
Blodgett, Joewilla, 37
Bloomer Girl (de Mille), 107
Boden(dorfer), Herman, 92, 118,
    119, 121, 123, 219, 221; quoted,
    98, 101
Bolero (LH), 54
Bolm, Adolph, 10-11
Bond, Carrie Jacobs, 22
Boogie Bali Woogie (LH), 105
Booth Theater, 30
Boroloff, Ivor, 24-25, 29
Borsch (recipe), 239
Borzoi Book of Modern Dance, The
    (Lloyd), 182, 195; quoted, 80-81
Bouquet For Molly, A (LH), 136,
    137
Bowne, William, 37, 42-44, 62, 63,
    65, 68, 70, 82, 94, 106, 109,
    112, 115, 119, 126, 134, 140,
    141, 145, 186, 194, 196;
    quoted, 50, 69, 135
Boynton, Constance, 49, 73
Bran, Mary, 155
Brazil, Indiana, 4, 10
Brigadoon (de Mille), 107
Brooks, David, 110
Brooks, Eleanor, 53, 62, 64, 92,
    219-221 *passim*
Brooks, Miriam, 219
Brown County, Indiana, 7
Brown County, Indiana (LH), 7, 9,
    145; (scenario), 228-230

Brown, Lew, 142
Burroughs, Bruce, 53
Butler, John, 91

Cadman, Charles Wakefield, 22, 31
California Ballet Company, 46
California, University of, 25, 27
"Caribbean Nights" (LH), 172
Carousel (de Mille), 107
Carter, Vernon, 195; quoted, 54
Case History No. – (Sokolow), 58
Cheney, Warren, 85
Children's Museum (Indianapolis),
    6, 7
"Choreo '50", 126, 137-139
"Choreo '51", 148, 150, 153, 156
"Choreo '52", 156, 167, 172
"Choreo '53", 172, 187
Climax (LH), 105
Coca, Imogene, 104
Cohen, Sol, 31
Collins, Janet, 128, 171, 181, 182
Conquest (LH), 86-88
Copland, Aaron, 121, 137
Cornick, Norman, 169, 176
Covington, Audree, 154
Cunningham, Merce, 86, 87, 185
Cutner, Sidney, 73, 75, 98

Dance in America, The (Terry), 53
Dance Magazine, 39, 95, 184, 195,
    197; quoted, 81, 143, 144, 185
Dance News, 197, 236; quoted, 185
Dance Observer, 39; quoted, 58
Dance of Parting (LH), 60
Dance Perspectives #31, 195, 196,
    197; quoted, 69, 79, 112-113,
    120-121, 168-169

Dance Repertory Group, 34
Dance Theater (Gould), 39, 45
Dance Theater (Horton), 43,
     115-120 *passim*, 128, 144, 145,
     147, 148, 149, 170
Dance Theater Company, 149
Dance Theater Contract, 240-241
Dance to the Piper (de Mille), 43
"Dancing Americans", 108
"Danzòn" (LH), 137, 139, 142
D'Arcy, Richard, 106, 169
Da Silva, Howard, 110
Dean, Harriet, 25, 27, 33
De Carlo, Yvonne, 136
Dedications in our Time (LH), 173
Dedication to José Clemente
     Orozco (LH), 155, 174, 185
De Haven, Rene, 154
de Lavallade, Carmen, 31, 53, 128,
     142, 145, 149, 150, 154, 156,
     167, 169, 170, 175, 185, 197;
     quoted, 143, 144
de Mille, Agnes, 43, 91, 107
Denby, Edwin, 104
Denishawn, 7, 9, 10, 20, 36, 48
Dictator (LH), 55, 61
Dilly Dali (LH), 108
Dodds, Jack, 149, 150, 154, 175,
     176
Donaldson, Donella (Julie Haydon),
     22
Dorn, Gerhardt, 89
Dudley, Alice, 106
Dvořak, Antonin, 16

Eagle Rock, California, 21, 29
Ebener (Rudko), Doris, 110
Educational Dance Magazine,
     quoted, 91, 201-211

Ellington, Duke, 165
El Robozo (LH), 137, 138, 139
Embolada (LH), 105
Eng, Frank, 61, 122, 147, 148, 157,
     170, 172, 174, 175, 181, 183,
     186-189 *passim*, 196, 197; quoted,
     125, 126, 168-169, 171
English, Bertha Miller, 47, 73, 81,
     85
Estilo De Tù (LH), 137
Excerpts From a War Poem
     (Sokolow), 59
Exhibition Dance No. 1 (LH), 74

Face of Violence (LH), 173, 175;
     (*see also Salome*)
Fairview Park, 14, 16
Farber, Malka, 106
Faubion, Jeri (Salkin), 53, 89, 92,
     142, 219, 220, 221
Feather of the Dawn, The
     (Shawn), 10
Fernandez, José, 85
Field Museum (Chicago), 16
Finch, Connie (Spriestersbach),
     119, 128, 134, 135
Finch, Keith, 135
Fisher, Nelle, 110
Flade, Tina, 39
Flight From Reality (LH), 61
Folies Bergère, 101, 103-105
Footlights Across America
     (Macgowan), 14, 193
Frankenstein, Alfred, 196;
     quoted, 86
"Frevo" (LH), 137
Frisco Sal (LH), 108
Fulton, June, 87
"Fun Dances", 148

Geiger, Miriam, 138, 196;
  quoted, 139
Georgi, Yvonne, 39
Gernreich, Rudi, 118, 123, 128,
  145; quoted, 231
Gerrard, Saida, 106
Gillanders, Dorothy, 87
Girl Crazy (LH), 156
Goldberg, Albert, 197; quoted,
  124, 125, 153, 166-167
Goldoni, Lelia, 31, 149, 169, 175
Goodrich, Val, 176
Gould, Norma, 38-39, 62, 112, 123
Goupil, Augie, 71
Graham, Martha, 8, 30, 39, 41, 59,
  79, 80, 91, 92, 155, 173, 181,
  184; quoted, 152
Green, Patricia, 37
Grunn, Homer, 10, 31, 51

Haggart, Stanley, 182
Harrison, Lou, 87, 88, 98;
  (letter), 232-235
Harrison, Ray, 110
Hassalevris, Constantine, 187,
  197, 236
Haven (LH), 84
Haydon, Julie, 22
Heasley, Maxine, 37
Hegyi, Viola (Swisher), 194, 196;
  quoted 51, 97
Hering, Doris, 184, 197; quoted,
  185
Herman, Dorothy, 87
Hewes, Theo, 8-9, 11, 14, 20
Heyden, Victor, 219
Hickman, Walter, 193; quoted, 9
Hollywood Bowl, 83

Hollywood Citizen News, quoted,
  51, 97
Holm, Hanya, 39, 86, 92
Holmes, Peggy, 106
"Hoop Dance" (LH), 60
Hoosiers, 5, 13
Horton, Annie Lauders
  (Poly Anna), 3, 4, 6, 10, 107-109
  passim, 187
Horton Ballets, 98
Horton Dance Group, 52, 61, 64,
  67, 69, 83, 85, 89, 92, 94, 95
Horton, Iredell, 3, 4, 6, 10, 107-109
  passim, 187
Horton, Lester, ancestors and
  parents, 3-4, 108-109, 187; as
  choreographer, 20, 33, 37, 38,
  45-52, 54-56, 60-62, 74-76,
  79-84, 86-89, 94-98, 105, 106,
  118, 120, 123, 125, 128, 134,
  135, 137-139, 142, 143-145, 148,
  150-155, 165-169, 173-175,
  183-184; quoted 72-73, 201-203,
  212-213; Chronology 243-255; as
  designer, 17, 20, 33, 38, 48-49,
  82, 166; as director, 35, 44, 172;
  as teacher, 17, 33-34, 35, 40-42,
  63, 66-67, 88, 90-92, 156-157,
  189-190, 231, 237, 238; and
  Bella Lewitzky, 62-63, 66, 105,
  107, 112-113, 140-142; childhood,
  3-7; Dance Theater years, 115-190;
  dance training, 7-11; education, 6,
  7, 9, 34; formative California
  years, 22-36; Horton Dance Group
  era, 52-105; illnesses, 32, 33, 109,
  145-148, 183, 190; Indiana years,
  5-20; in New York, 103-104,
  181-182; interest in American

(Horton, Lester)
  Indians, 6-7, 8, 9, 17, 19, 22, 25,
  26, 27, 29-30, 60, 120, 183-184,
  204-211; work in films, 98, 101,
  105, 108, 111, 136, 172, 186;
  Film Chronology, 255; work in
  musical comedy, 109-110,
  155-156, 252
Horton-Wagner Group, 34
House Un-American Activities
  Committee, 61
Humphrey, Doris, 8, 39, 173, 181,
  184
Humphrey-Weidman, 41, 80
Hungerford, Mary Jane, 96
Hurok, Sol, 95, 155

Indiana Centennial Pageant, 12, 17
Indiana Prize Plays (Bates), 13
Indianapolis Little Theatre, 11-14,
  17, 19
Indianapolis Star, The, 11
Indianapolis Theatre Guild, 13, 14,
  16, 31
Indianapolis Times, The, 193;
  quoted, 9
International Folk Dance Festival,
  118
Introduction to the Dance
  (lecture-demonstration), 88
Ishtar of the Seven Gates
  (St. Denis), 10
Ito, Michio, 30-31, 40, 48, 85

Jacob's Pillow, 186, 188
Jaques-Dalcroze, Emile, 30
Jenkins, William E., 11

John Herron Art Institute, 12, 18,
  20
Johns, Erik, 123
Johnson, Eleanor (Elle), 149, 167
Jones, Isabel Morse, 194, 196;
  quoted, 49, 51, 82, 84, 85, 94,
  212-213
Jowitt, Deborah, 197; quoted, 174

Katzell, William, 104-106
Kawasumi, Misaye, 149, 170, 173,
  175
Kenton, Stan, 152, 153
King, Helen W., 95, 195; quoted, 81
King, Madolyn, 34
Kirkpatrick, Nathan, 110
Kirpich, Billie, 110
Klaus, Kenneth, 174
Kline, William, 44, 47
Koch, Frederick, 13, 14
Koerner, Martha, 176
Kolodney, William, 171, 182
Kootenai War Dance (LH), 37
Kreck, Luisa, 128, 134, 137, 142,
  156
Kreutzberg, Harald, 92
Kulberg, Jessie, 183
Kurgans, Ana, 53
Kurtz, Efrem, 83
Kuuks Walks Alone, 53

Lady in the Sack, The (Seiler), 35
Lawrence, Florence, 194; quoted,
  51
Lee, Robert Tyler, 89
Lesser, Sol, 172

Lester Horton Dancers, The, 36
105, 118, 149
Lewitzky, Bella, 31, 53, 54, 61-64,
65, 75, 81, 82, 87, 88, 92, 105,
106, 107, 111, 112, 115, 118,
121, 123, 125, 136-144 *passim*,
195, 196, 219, 220, 221;
quoted, 41, 50, 63, 69, 71, 74,
79, 120
Liberian Suite (LH), 165-167
Limón, Jośe, 181
Lind, Betty, 106
Little Review, 20, 25, 27
Little Theater of the Verdugos, 35,
37, 38, 44, 53, 68
Lloyd, Margaret, 195, 197; quoted,
80, 182
Lober, David, 92, 221
Lorca, Garcia, 167
Los Angeles County Drama
Association, 35, 44
Los Angeles Daily News, The, 196;
quoted, 125, 138
Los Angeles Examiner, The, 197;
quoted, 51
*Los Angeles Herald and Express,
The*, 135, 195; quoted, 55, 81, 93
Los Angeles Record, The, 195;
quoted, 54
Los Angeles Times, The, 196, 197;
quoted, 49, 50, 51, 82, 84, 85,
95, 124, 125, 130, 153, 167,
212-213
Los Angeles Tribune, The, 138,
196; quoted, 126, 139
Lyons, James, 87
Lysistrata (LH), 75, 97, 154

MacDermott, Adrian, 219
Macgowan, Kenneth, quoted, 14

Magic Island, The (Seabrook), 37
Manchester, P.W., 197; quoted,
175, 185
Maracci, Carmelita, 92, 144,
170-171, 182
Martin, Don, 128
Martin, John, 75, 171, 185, 197;
quoted, 190
Martinez, Elsie, 25, 33, 194;
quoted, 26-27
Martinez, Guadelupe, 219
Martinez, Michaela, 25
Martinez, Xavier, 25, 27
Masarachia, Toni, 49, 51, 193;
quoted, 5
Mason, Redfern, 194; quoted, 23
May Night (LH), 45, 60, 61, 62
Medea (LH), 153-155
Medea (Jeffers), 153
Mensendieck, Dr. Bess, 66
Menzeli, Madame, 8
Metz, Anita (Grossman), 118
Meyer, Mary, 53
Mills College, 86, 96
Mine, The (LH), 55
Mitchell, James, 66, 92, 106, 107,
185, 219, 221
Moncion, Francisco, 110
Montandon, Joy (Montaya), 47, 49,
62
Moonlight in Havana (LH), 98
Morrow, Doretta, 110
Mound Builders (LH), 55, 174
Murat Theater, 7, 10

Nashville Civic Ballet, 10
Nathan, George Jean, 22

"New Dance Explained as
Evolution" (article), 212-213
New Dance League, 57
New York Herald Tribune, The,
197; quoted, 184
New York Post, The, 195;
quoted, 57, 59
New York Times, The, 197;
quoted, 190
Nichols, Ethel, 53, 75
Nielson, Lavina, 110
Nikolais, Alwin, 185
Ninety-Second Street YM-YWHA,
171, 181, 186
Noble Comedy, A (LH), 97 (*see
also Lysistrata*)

Ojai Music Festival, 153
Oliver, W.E., 194, 195; quoted, 51,
55, 81, 93
Olympic Festival of Dance, 36
On the Upbeat (LH), 150-151
Orans, Sondra, 128, 137
Orozco, José Clemente, 26, 87

Painted Desert Ballet (LH), 51
Painter, Hazel (Mrs. Robert), 3
Paramount Theater, 37
Park, The (LH), 134, 138, 145
Parks, Bernice, 110
Parnes, Irwin, 118
Pasaremos (LH), 84
Pavley-Oukrainsky School, 11
Pavlova, Anna, 8
Perkins, Ed, 46, 47,52
Phantom of the Opera (LH), 98
Philharmonic Auditorium, 80

Pierre, Dorathi Bock, 64, 196;
quoted, 54, 84
Pinwheel (Ito), 30
Poetry Magazine, 20
Prado de Pena (LH), 167, 168, 170,
183, 184
Pratt, Steve, 219
Press, Jacques, 98
Prologue to an Earth Celebration
(LH), 85

Rain Quest (LH), 60
Rains, Claude, 98
Rapoport, Leon (Paul Steffen), 92,
219, 221
Ratcliff, Carl, 118, 120, 128, 137,
138
Reed, Susan, 110
Revelations (Ailey), 37
Reynolds, Newell, 92, 97, 112,
118-120, 128, 139, 140, 141, 171
Rhythm Section (LH), 145, 165
Richards, Myra, 19
Rite of Spring, The (LH), *see Sacre
du Printemps, Le*
Robbins, Jerome, 91
Robinson, Earl, 137
Robinson, Gertrude Rivers, 167,
185
Rogers, Will, Jr., 82
Roots of the Blues (Ailey), 134
Ross, Herbert, 110

Sacre du Printemps, Le (LH),
83-84, 165; (program notes),
215-218
Safier, Loys, 37
Salkin, Leo, 89, 121

Salome (LH), 46-50, 52, 75, 81, 82, 85, 86, 121, 122, 128, 142, 144-145, 172, 173; *see also Face of Violence*

Salome, Where She Danced (LH), 108

San Francisco Chronicle, The, 195; quoted, 86

San Francisco Examiner, The, 194; quoted, 23

Santa Cruz, Domingo, 98

Schindler, R.M., 116

Scott, Raymond, 98

Seabrook, W.B., 37

Second Gnossienne (LH), 60

Selleck, Roda, 9

7 Scenes With Ballabilli (LH), 167, 172

Shady Lady (LH), 108

Shaw, Sonia, 104, 106, 110

Shawn, Ted, 7, 8, 10, 21, 39, 51, 186

Shootin' Star (LH), 109-110

Shortridge High School, 7, 9

Shostakovich, Dimitri, 98

Shrine Auditorium, 46

Shurman, Nona, 110

Shurr, Gertrude, 156

Silver, Lilyan, 190

Sixteen to Twenty-Four (LH), 96

Smith, Darr, quoted 138

Sokolow, Anna, 58, 59

"Soldadera" (LH), 137, 139, 142, 175

Something to Please Everybody (LH), 92, 96, 98, 106, 137; (spoken commentary), 221-224

Somnes, George, 13

Song of Hiawatha, The, 15, 17-25, 34

Song of Quetzalcoatl (Harrison), 88

South Sea Woman (LH), 186

Spector, Frances, 123

St. Denis, Ruth, 7, 8, 10, 118, 197; quoted, 186

Steele, T.C., 15

Stuart Walker Stock Company, 13

Stubergh, Katherine, 43, 69, 103, 194; quoted, 23, 32, 33

Svedrovsky, Henry, 83

Swisher, Viola, *see* Hegyi, Viola

Takwish, The Star Maker (LH), 38

Talbot-Martin, Elizabeth, 37, 49, 62, 194; quoted, 45

Tales of Hoffman, 108

Tangier (LH), 111

Tarkington, Booth, 15

Taylor, Blair, 19

Terry, Walter, 53, 197; quoted, 184

Tetley, Glen, 91

That Night With You (LH), 108

Theater Journal, 195; quoted, 72

Thornburg, Forrest, 10

3-D Follies (LH), 172

Tierra Y Libertad! (LH), 88, 92, 98, 106; (program notes), 219-220

"To José Clemente Orozco", *see Dedication to José Clemente Orozco*

Tootikian, Karoun, 37, 194; quoted, 36

Tootikian, Lavallete, 37

Totem Incantation (LH), 120-121

Touch of Klee and Delightful 2, A (LH), 128, 139

Trisler, Joyce, 31, 149, 169, 173, 174, 176, 197; quoted, 66, 188, 189-190

Tropic Trio (LH), 150
Truitte, James, 53, 149, 154, 167, 169, 170, 174-176 *passim,* 186, 197; quoted, 151, 237-238

Udane, Edythe, 110
Universal International Studios, 98, 105, 108
University of Southern California, 96

van Cleve, Kita, 53, 81, 92, 182
van den Berg, Brahm, 37, 49, 52, 63, 92, 121
Victory Ball Waltz (LH), 105
Villa-Lobos, Heitor, 98
Village Voice, The, 197; quoted, 174
Voodoo Ceremonial (LH), 37, 45, 51

Wagner, Dorothy, 34
Wallace, General Lew, 6, 19
Warsaw Ghetto (LH), 134, 135
Weidman, Charles, 8
White Jade (St. Denis), 118
White Savage (LH), 98
Whittaker, Herman, 26
Wigman, Mary, 36, 41, 48
Wilde, Oscar, 44, 123
Woodbury, Portia (Bowne), 37, 48, 126, 186

"Xango" (LH), 137, 142
Xochitl (Shawn), 7, 51

Yeats, William Butler, 31, 134
Yokom, Rachael, 156

Zemach, Benjamin, 67

Lester Horton was the greatest influence of my career. He is the reason I do all this. He was a genius at the theatre. Besides being a major choreographer he was a master costume designer, master painter, master sculptor. An incredible man . . . . When you came into the world of Lester Horton you came into a completely creative environment—people of all colors, music of all nations . . . .

From an Interview with Alvin Ailey by Moira Hodgson in *Dance News—* April 1976.

about the author . . .

Larry Warren received both his B.A. and M.A. in dance from U.C.L.A. Evening-long chats with Ruth St. Denis in the tiny patio behind her California studio triggered his interest in Dance History and Research, which he later pursued in graduate courses with John Martin at U.C.L.A. He has taught at Eugene Loring's American School of Dance, Immaculate Heart College in Los Angeles, and the University of Wisconsin. He is presently Associate Professor of Dance at the University of Maryland and Director of Maryland Dance Theater.